COMPREHENSIVE RESEARCH
AND STUDY GUIDE

BLOOM'S MAJOR SHORT STORY WRITERS

Katherine Anne Porter

EDITED AND WITH AN
INTRODUCTION BY HAROLD BLOOM

BLOOM'S MAJOR SHORT STORY WRITERS

Anton Chekhov
Joseph Conrad
Stephen Crane
William Faulkner
F. Scott Fitzgerald
Nathaniel Hawthorne
Ernest Hemingway
O. Henry
Shirley Jackson
Henry James
James Joyce
D. H. Lawrence
Jack London
Herman Melville
Flannery O'Connor
Edgar Allan Poe
Katherine Anne Porter
J. D. Salinger
John Steinbeck
Mark Twain
John Updike
Eudora Welty

BLOOM'S MAJOR WORLD POETS

Maya Angelou
Robert Browning
Geoffrey Chaucer
Samuel T. Coleridge
Dante
Emily Dickinson
John Donne
T. S. Eliot
Robert Frost
Homer
Langston Hughes
John Keats
John Milton
Sylvia Plath
Edgar Allan Poe
Poets of World War I
Shakespeare's Poems & Sonnets
Percy Shelley
Alfred, Lord Tennyson
Walt Whitman
William Wordsworth
William Butler Yeats

COMPREHENSIVE RESEARCH
AND STUDY GUIDE

BLOOM'S
MAJOR
SHORT STORY
WRITERS

Katherine Anne

Porter

EDITED AND WITH AN INTRODUCTION BY HAROLD BLOOM

Printed and bound in the United States of America.

First Printing
1 3 5 7 9 8 6 4 2

Library of Congress Cataloging-in-Publication Data
Katherine Anne Porter / edited by Harold Bloom.
        p. cm. — (Bloom's major short story writers)
    Includes bibliographical references and index.
    ISBN 0-7910-5941-3
      1. Porter, Katherine Anne, 1890–1980—Criticism and interpretation.
    2. Women and literature—United States—History—20th century.
    3. Short story. I. Bloom, Harold. II. Series.

    PS3531.O752 Z69 2000
    813'.52—dc21   00-024064

Chelsea House Publishers
1974 Sproul Road, Suite 400
Broomall, PA 19008-0914

The Chelsea House World Wide Web address is
http://www.chelseahouse.com

Contributing Editor: Aaron Tillman

Produced by Robert Gerson Publisher's Services, Avondale, PA

Contents

User's Guide

This volume is designed to present biographical, critical, and bibliographical information on the author's best-known or most important short stories. Following Harold Bloom's editor's note and introduction is a detailed biography of the author, discussing major life events and important literary accomplishments. A plot summary of each short story follows, tracing significant themes, patterns, and motifs in the work, and an annotated list of characters supplies brief information on the main characters in each story.

A selection of critical extracts, derived from previously published material from leading critics, analyzes aspects of each short story. The extracts consist of statements from the author, if available, early reviews of the work, and later evaluations up to the present. A bibliography of the author's writings (including a complete list of all books written, cowritten, edited, and translated), a list of additional books and articles on the author and the work, and an index of themes and ideas in the author's writings conclude the volume.

～

Harold Bloom is Sterling Professor of the Humanities at Yale University and Henry W. and Albert A. Berg Professor of English at the New York University Graduate School. He is the author of over 20 books, including *Shelley's Mythmaking* (1959), *The Visionary Company* (1961), *Blake's Apocalypse* (1963), *Yeats* (1970), *A Map of Misreading* (1975), *Kabbalah and Criticism* (1975), *Agon: Toward a Theory of Revisionism* (1982), *The American Religion* (1992), *The Western Canon* (1994), and *Omens of Millennium: The Gnosis of Angels, Dreams, and Resurrection* (1996). *The Anxiety of Influence* (1973) sets forth Professor Bloom's provocative theory of the literary relationships between the great writers and their predecessors. His most recent books include *Shakespeare: The Invention of the Human,* a 1998 National Book Award finalist, and *How to Read and Why,* which was published in 2000.

Professor Bloom earned his Ph.D. from Yale University in 1955 and has served on the Yale faculty since then. He is a 1985 MacArthur Foundation Award recipient, served as the Charles Eliot Norton Professor of Poetry at Harvard University in 1987–88, and has received honorary degrees from the universities of Rome and Bologna. In 1999, Professor Bloom received the prestigious American Academy of Arts and Letters Gold Medal for Criticism.

Currently, Harold Bloom is the editor of numerous Chelsea House volumes of literary criticism, including the series BLOOM'S NOTES, BLOOM'S MAJOR DRAMATISTS, BLOOM'S MAJOR NOVELISTS, MAJOR LITERARY CHARACTERS, MODERN CRITICAL VIEWS, MODERN CRITICAL INTERPRETATIONS, and WOMEN WRITERS OF ENGLISH AND THEIR WORKS.

Editor's Note

My Introduction broods upon "Flowering Judas" as Porter's vision of her own incarnation as a storyteller.

As there are twenty-five critical extracts covering four stories, I call attention here only to a few that I have found particularly useful.

Thomas F. Walsh illuminates the origins of "Flowering Judas," while Darlene Harbour Unrue traces the sources and influences that helped created "Old Mortality."

"Pale Horse, Pale Rider" is related to Porter's Texas background by Janis P. Stout, after which John Edward Hardy finds in "The Grave" a Wordsworthian sense of natural piety.

Introduction

HAROLD BLOOM

All four of the stories by Katherine Anne Porter that are discussed in this volume seem to me aesthetic triumphs, but I retain my lifelong preference for "Flowering Judas," though it is less subtle than her other major achievements. The high rhetoric of "Flowering Judas" owes something to T. S. Eliot's "Gerontion," and has the same relation to Eliot—a revisionary critique—as do some of the greater lyrics of Hart Crane, whose self-destructiveness in Mexico was powerfully described by Porter. Though Porter's prime narrative precursor was Henry James, she had a kind of inverse affinity to D. H. Lawrence, who is also revised, rather cunningly, in "Flowering Judas," which is at once a spellbinding prose poem and what Frank O'Connor called "a pure story," rather than "an applied story," as in a novel.

In "Flowering Judas" Laura is a virgin, holding herself back from the sexual maelstrom of the Mexican revolution, in which she is a political participant. Yet this virginity is, in itself, a profoundly sexual state of being, provocative not only to her Mexican male companions but to Laura herself, narcissistically preoccupied with her own beauty and with her own burgeoning sensibility as an artist.

D. H. Lawrence, in the sublime madness of his Mexican novel *The Plumed Serpent,* was outrageously misogynistic, and "Flowering Judas" makes a strong, implicit response to Lawrence. The story's heroine is a survivor, preserving herself in the interest of her own art. Lawrence would have reacted to Laura with a singular fury, as perhaps William Blake might have done also, for Laura certainly incarnates what they rejected as the Female Will. And there is something destructive in Laura's being; she is, involuntarily, a fatal woman:

> A brown, shock-haired youth came and stood in her patio one night and sang like a lost soul for two hours, but Laura could think of nothing to do about it. The moonlight spread a wash of gauzy silver over the clear spaces of the garden, and the shadows were cobalt blue. The scarlet blossoms of the Judas tree were dull purple, and the names of the colors repeated themselves automatically in her mind, while she watched not the boy, but his shadow fallen like a dark garment across the fountain rim, trailing in the water.

For Laura, the boy himself is only a shadow, but why should he not be? Laura is a portrait of the artist as a young woman, about to cross over into the exercise of her own art. Her narcissism is the artist's necessary defense against experience, particularly against an all-consuming eros. In Lawrence, Laura would become *materia poetica*, a sacrifice to Lawrence's prophetic vision. Katherine Anne Porter, poised upon the threshold of her own downward path to wisdom, holds Laura back from too premature a bright destruction. ❀

Biography of
Katherine Anne Porter

Katherine Anne Porter was born Callie Russell Porter on May 15, 1890, in Indian Creek, Texas, to Harrison and Mary Alice Jones Porter. Two years later, Callie's mother passed away and the family moved to Kyle, Texas, to live with Harrison's mother, Catherine Anne Porter. In 1901 Harrison's mother died. Soon after her death, Harrison sold his mother's farm and moved his family to San Antonio, Texas, where Callie attended several different private schools.

When Callie was sixteen she ran away from home and married John Henry Koontz. They were divorced three years later, in 1909. In 1911, she went to Chicago where she worked at a newspaper and as a bit player for a film company. Soon after, Callie moved back to Texas and changed her name to Katherine Anne Porter. In 1915 she contracted tuberculosis. She spent the next few years in and out of hospitals and sanitariums.

In 1917, having recovered from her illness, she became a writer for *The Critic*, a Fort Worth weekly newspaper. Nearly two years later she got a job as a reporter for *The Rocky Mountain News* in Denver. She became critically ill with influenza, but survived; after her recovery, she moved to New York and supported herself by working for a motion picture magazine, writing stories for children, and preparing a libretto for a Mexican ballet.

In 1920 she traveled to Mexico to study art and was witness to the Obregon revolution. The following year she returned to Fort Worth and wrote articles about Mexico, as well as her first recognized story, "Maria Concepcion." In 1922 she returned to Mexico to help prepare an exhibit of folk art. Soon after she returned to New York, where she worked on a biography of Cotton Mather and wrote book reviews for various periodicals.

In 1930 Porter's first collection of fiction, *Flowering Judas, and Other Stories,* was published. Following this publication she received a Guggenheim fellowship and moved to Mexico. In August of 1931, she sailed to Europe aboard a German ship. The journal she wrote during this voyage provided the basic material for *Ship of Fools.*

In 1933 Porter married Eugene Pressly of the U.S. Foreign Service. After the marriage the couple moved to Paris, where she published a book of French songs with translations, *Katherine Anne Porter's French Song Book*. The following year she published "Hacienda," not long before an enlarged edition of *Flowering Judas, and Other Stories* was released. In 1937 she received a Book-of-the-Month Club award for *Noon Wine*. Later that same year she divorced Eugene Pressly.

Porter married Albert Erskine Jr., a member of the faculty at Louisiana State University, in 1938. Later that year she received her second Guggenheim Fellowship. In 1939 her widely acclaimed book of three short novels, *Pale Horse, Pale Rider*, was published. The following year, she received the first annual gold medal for literature from the Society of Libraries of New York University for her collection of short novels.

In 1942 she published a translation, with introduction, of Jose Joaquin Fernandez de Lizardi's *The Itching Parrot*. Later that same year she divorced Albert Erskine Jr. In 1943 she was elected a member of the National Institute of Arts and Letters. The following year *The Leaning Tower, and Other Stories,* was published.

In 1949 she accepted the first of several appointments as a writer-in-residence and guest lecturer, this time at Stanford University. She would later hold similar positions at the University of Chicago, University of Michigan, and University of Virginia. In 1952 she published *The Days Before*. In 1959 she received a Ford Foundation grant in literature.

Three years after receiving the Ford Foundation grant she received an O. Henry Memorial award for "Holiday." Within that same year she published *Ship of Fools*, which was a Book-of-the-Month Club selection and a best-seller, and received an Emerson-Thoreau Bronze Medal from the American Academy of Arts and Sciences.

In 1965 *The Collected Stories of Katherine Anne Porter* was published. The following year she received the Pulitzer Prize and the National Book Award for fiction. In 1967 she published *A Christmas Story*. Three years later *The Collected Essays and Occasional Writings of Katherine Anne Porter* was published. In 1977 she published *The Never-Ending Wrong*.

Katherine Anne Porter died on September 18, 1980, in Silver Spring, Maryland. Her body was cremated and her ashes were buried at Indian Creek, Texas. ❀

Plot Summary of
"Flowering Judas"

Flowering Judas, one of Katherine Anne Porter's most acclaimed stories, opens in Mexico as Braggioni, an influential leader in the Mexican revolution, is playing guitar and singing painfully off-key to Laura, the principle character in the story. Since the commencement of Braggioni's courting ritual, Laura has looked for ways to avoid her own home. She lives with Lupe, an Indian maid, who warns her whenever her suitor is waiting.

As the story progresses, the reader is made aware of the power and influence that Braggioni weilds among the revolutionaries and his subsequent cruelty toward those who do not respect him. Laura is the exception, though she does earn part of her living running errands for Braggioni.

Laura came to Mexico with certain preconceived, romanticized ideas about the revolution and the makeup of a genuine revolutionary. These notions have been shattered by the crude manners and "gluttonous bulk" of Braggioni, who has become a "symbol of her many disillusions." Porter characterizes Laura as a person who "has been betrayed irreparably by the disunion between her way of living and her feeling of what life should be." Braggioni claims that she was bred for disappointment.

Since Laura's decision to come to Mexico she has been living in a state of inaction. She feels she has committed herself to a life different from what she had imagined. And now she is left to suffer in her disunity. She spends her days teaching English to devoted Indian children and her evenings and portions of her leisure time visiting "prisoners of her own political faith." She brings them food, cigarettes, money, and narcotics—items to make their time in jail easier. She also brings word from Braggioni, whom the prisoners consider the great hope of the revolution.

Laura runs many chores for Braggioni and accumulates a number of suitors, none of whom can figure out why she is in Mexico. One of the suitors is a captain in Zapata's army. He attempts, as they ride horses together, to express his love for her but she spurs her horse at the moment he expresses his affection and both horses gallop off.

Another suitor is a boy who serenades Laura from her patio. She gives him a dollar, upon the suggestion of Lupe, to get him to leave. What she does not realize is that he would come back each ensuing evening to serenade her and leave poems for her.

Laura uses her stoicism and isolation to combat the regret and fear that come with her current situation. She feels like a stranger in the world, teaching strangers, passing notes to strangers, and earning a livelihood from a person whom she never wishes to know. She has lived twenty-two years without getting close to anyone. She is a virgin, with great beauty, who uses distance and denial for strength and protection.

The narrative lingers on Braggioni, touching on his past life as a poet without concern for the revolution, and contrasting this former self with his present position as a ruthless revolutionary hero. He has left his wife to seek out the company of Laura. She envies Braggioni's wife for her ability to weep and express true grief over a concrete cause. During a break from his guitar playing, Braggioni asks Laura why she has chosen to take part in a revolution that is not her own. He questions whether she is in love with someone who is fighting for the revolutionary cause. She claims that she is not.

As the narrative moves back into dialogue, Laura reveals to Braggioni that Eugenio, one of the prisoners to whom Laura delivers messages and narcotics, has overdosed and died. Braggioni expresses no remorse, calling him a fool who could not wait to be saved.

Laura senses a change in Braggioni's voice and suspects that she might not see him for a while. Her suspicions are correct as he returns to his wife that evening. Braggioni's wife has spent hours each night sobbing over the absence of her beloved husband. Braggioni weeps with his wife who then washes his feet and restates her devotion to him.

That night Laura goes to sleep thinking about Eugenio, the deceased prisoner. He comes to her in a dream and tells her to follow him. She says she will follow only if he offers his hand to her. This moment is significant as Laura has been devoted, up to that point, to her own isolation, refraining from reaching out to anyone. Eugenio claims to be taking her to Death. He refuses to offer up his hand and calls her a murderer and a prisoner.

Eugenio rips the flowers off a Judas tree and presses them against Laura's lips. She discovers that his hand and his body are not made of flesh. She eats the flowers, satisfying her hunger and her thirst. The story ends, at the end of Laura's dream, with a haunting exchange of Eugenio's claims and Laura's cries: "Murderer! said Eugenio, and Cannibal! This is my body and my blood. Laura cried No! and at the sound of her own voice, she awoke trembling, and was afraid to sleep again." ❀

List of Characters in
"Flowering Judas"

Braggioni is the first character the reader encounters. He is an influential leader in the Mexican Revolution. He spends nights playing guitar and singing for Laura. He sends Laura to the jail houses and various parts of town to deliver messages and narcotics to his followers.

Laura is the principal character in the story. She is an American who has moved to Mexico to take part in the revolution. She is not sure why she is there nor what she hopes to accomplish. She gains strength in her stoicism and isolation. She teaches English to Mexican children during the day and runs errands for Braggioni at night.

Lupe is an Indian maid who lives with Laura. She tells Laura when Braggioni is waiting for her.

Eugenio was a revolutionary who spent time in prison. He died of an overdose of narcotics in his cell. He appears in Laura's dream toward the end of the story and calls her a murderer and a prisoner. ❀

Critical Views on
"Flowering Judas"

THOMAS F. WALSH ON THE MAKING OF THE STORY

[Thomas F. Walsh was a professor of English at Georgetown University. His articles on Katherine Anne Porter have appeared in *American Literature,* the *Georgia Review,* and elsewhere. He is the author of *Katherine Anne Porter and Mexico: The Illusion of Eden.* In this excerpt, Walsh discusses Porter's inspiration for the story.]

Porter's earliest comment on "Flowering Judas" appeared in 1942:

> The idea came to me one evening when going to visit the girl I call Laura in the story. I passed the open window of her living room on my way to the door, through the small patio which is one of the scenes in the story. I had a brief glimpse of her sitting with an open book in her lap, but not reading, with a fixed look of pained melancholy and confusion in her face. The fat man I call Braggioni was playing the guitar and singing to her.

Porter "thought" she understood "the desperate complications" of the girl's mind and feelings, but if she did not know "her true story," she did know a story "that seemed symbolic truth." In subsequent interviews Porter gave the expanded versions of the "small seed" from which her story grew. In 1963 she added the Judas tree and identified the girl as her friend "Mary" who was teaching in an Indian school and "was not able to take care of herself, because she was not able to face her own nature and was afraid of everything." In 1965 Porter added the fountain and insisted that the small apartment where "Mary Doherty" lived alone was exactly as it appears in the story. Doherty, whom a young *Zapatista* captain attempted to help from her horse, was a "virtuous, intact, strait-laced Irish Catholic . . . born with the fear of sex," who had asked Porter to sit with her because she was not sure of the man coming to sing to her. This Porter did, outwaiting him until he left in frustration. She refused to identify the man, stating that she rolled "four or five objectionable characters into one" to create Braggioni. She also claimed she was like the girl in the story, taking "messages to people living in dark alleys." A few years later she added that she visited political prisoners in their cells, two of whom she named. In a lecture taped at the University of Maryland in 1972, Porter gave the fullest and least reliable account of her story's genesis, stating that both she and Doherty brought food and sleeping pills to political prisoners, one of whom persuaded Doherty to give him fifty pills with which he killed himself. When Doherty reported the man's death to "Braggioni," he told her they were well rid of him. Later she dreamed that when she refused the attempt of "Eugenio" to lead her to death, "he gave her the flowering Judas buds." "This is her dream," Porter claimed, adding, "You see, my fiction is reportage, only I do something to it; I arrange it and it is fiction, but it happened." In a film made at the University of Maryland in 1976, she stated that Doherty should have known better than to give pills to the prisoner and, for the first time, gave Yúdico as Braggioni's model. As Porter added details about "Flowering Judas" over the years, reality more and more resembled what grew out of it, the story becoming "reportage," mainly of the actions and motives of Mary Doherty, about whom Porter could only speculate in 1942. Porter did indeed "arrange" reality to make it fiction, both in the creation of her story and in her versions of that creation. Her story is "based on real persons and events," but not as in her versions.

—Thomas F. Walsh, "The Making of 'Flowering Judas,'" *Journal of Modern Literature* 12, no. 1 (March 1985): pp. 109–11.

James T. F. Tanner on Laura

[James T. F. Tanner is a professor of English at the University of North Texas. His works include *The Texas Legacy of Katherine Anne Porter*. In this excerpt, Tanner discusses the unique attributes of Laura, the principal character in the story.]

"Flowering Judas," considered by many critics one of the greatest of American short stories, and by most Porter critics as her finest production in that genre, appears in all major American short story collections. In this story, for a change, it is the female who is passive (it would seem), the male dominant (after a fashion), though it can be seen that Laura's passivity is in this case a survival strategy and is very close in fact to dominance.

In her role as a revolutionary, Laura is the passive being in a man's world, both consciously and unconsciously catering to the world of masculine urges to power and dominance; thus she is a "Judas" figure in full bloom as the story unfolds. Her fear of Braggioni, in reality her fear of obliteration, causes her to cater to his smallest wishes—except his desire for sexual relations, that sacrifice apparently reserved as a last resort to protect her life. As long as she can say "No" to sexuality, so long does she have something of value that can be bartered for her continued existence. That Laura may eventually be required to surrender even her sexual integrity to Braggioni is strongly suggested in Porter's masterful use of the pistol (a transparent phallic symbol), which Laura is required to clean and polish, and which Braggioni strokes, ever so gently, while it lies in her lap. Reinforcing the theme of the inevitable sexual surrender of Laura to Braggioni is her willingness to listen to Braggioni's singing, despite the fact that she is bored to tears, while he "curves his swollen fingers around the throat of the guitar and softly smothers the music out of it" and "scratches" a miserable melody from the instrument, a foreshadowing of the inevitable rape/violation/seduction awaiting her, a consummation, however, that may not necessarily spell her destruction. The counterplay of pistol and guitar set the threatening, ominous stage; but Laura is something of a stage manager. As the desirable female, yet a woman traitorous to conventional womanhood, power lurks in her being. While nothing good is promised for Laura, and though her passivity assures her continued desirability, she treads a dangerous course.

Laura's essential treason is that she is being *used* for the purpose of others; she is not actively or passionately *engaged* in the revolutionary enterprise. Like the original Judas, she has sold out. She is not *really* Catholic, only Catholic in name, but she knows how to manipulate the trappings and symbolic rigmarole of the Church (like any good creative artist who finds Catholic symbol more useful than barren Protestant motif). She is not *really* aristocratic, but a desire for lace that is not machine-made suggests that she aims at standards for herself that she would not struggle to achieve for others; here she resembles the erotic Braggioni who loves his yellow silk handkerchiefs, "Jockey Club, imported from New York." Her Marxism, like that of Braggioni, is purely for show; it is a way to walk within the corridors of power. She, like Braggioni, proves quite capable of administering the death penalty; like the survivor that she essentially is, she will continue on this dangerous path.

—James T. F. Tanner, *The Texas Legacy of Katherine Anne Porter* (Denton: University of North Texas Press, 1990): pp. 140–42.

THOMAS F. WALSH ON ALIENATION

[Thomas F. Walsh was a professor of English at Georgetown University. His articles on Katherine Anne Porter have appeared in *American Literature,* the *Georgia Review,* and elsewhere. He is the author of *Katherine Anne Porter and Mexico: The Illusion of Eden.* In this excerpt, Walsh describes the story as one of cultural alienation. Quotes in this essay, except where noted, are from *The Collected Stories of Katherine Anne Porter.*]

The ultimate story of cultural alienation is, of course, "Flowering Judas." A "*gringuita*" to Braggioni, Laura rejects "knowledge and kinship" with all, including her students, who "remain strangers to her." She goes on "errands into strange streets, to speak to the strange faces that will appear." Finding no pleasure in "remembering her life before she came" to Mexico, she cannot imagine living in "another country." She is indeed countryless, her estrangement reaching metaphysical proportions in that "she is not at home in the world." At the end of the story, she is like a ghost, attired in "a white linen nightgown," who dreams of Eugenio's invitation to leave "this strange house" and join him in a "new country" of death. The ghost image suggests estrangement in time as well as space, with Porter's characters returning to a place as if from the grave and discovering that they do not belong there. In "Holiday," Ottilie moved among her family "as invisible to their imaginations as a ghost." In "Noon Wine," Helton, "a stranger in a strange land," is like a "disembodied spirit," who speaks "as from the tomb." At the end of "Old Mortality," Miranda, alienated from her family, thinks, "It is I who have no place. . . . Where are my own people and my own time?" Like her dead Aunt Amy, whom she resembles in temperament, Miranda is a ghost just as her aunt was only "a ghost in a frame" to her.

"Flowering Judas" shows that Porter, feeling cut off from her own family and her Texas past, discovered in the foreign culture of Mexico total estrangement, just as she had discovered there perfect Edenic bliss. Although she once described Mexico as her "familiar country" ⟨in *The Collected Essays and Occasional Writings of Katherine Anne Porter*⟩, her alter ego in "The Grave" moves, like Laura, through "a strange city of a strange country." And yet Porter clung to the "permanent hope" that she would find her place. That hope struggled against despair, fueling her imagination and shaping her fiction. Only there and in death could she return to her "loved and never-forgotten country."

—Thomas F. Walsh, "From Texas to Mexico to Texas," in *Katherine Anne Porter and Texas: An Uneasy Relationship*, eds. Clinton Machann and William Bedford Clark (College Station: Texas A&M University Press, 1990): pp. 82–83.

PETER G. CHRISTENSEN ON CRITICISM OF LAURA

[Peter G. Christensen has taught English at Marquette University. His specialty is twentieth-century comparative literature and film. He has written articles on Jean Toomer, John Rollin Ridge, Thorton Wilder, and Washington Irving. In this excerpt, Christensen speaks on the unduly harsh criticism of the main character in the story.]

Before comparing the themes common to both Porter and Lawrence, we should note that most criticism of "Flowering Judas" has been unduly harsh on the protagonist Laura. Ever since Porter commented on Laura's "self-delusion" ("Why She Selected 'Flowering Judas'"), critics have not been hesitant to show a number of other failings in her. Unfortunately, many of these failings tell more about the critic than about the story, and a fairer evaluation of Laura would show her to have an emotional paralysis caused by an extremely difficult social situation, including conflicting loyalties.

The much-noted symbols in the story have been used against Laura. Since they carry such a heavy weight, it is possible to lose one's sense of proportion in thinking how the events in question actually affect her or reveal her character. Three instances can illustrate this. Laura's dream of Eugenio should not be read as a dream which symbolizes a real state of affairs. As Dorothy Redden has held, it is an anxiety dream. Although Laura had given Eugenio the drugs he had used to commit suicide, this had been his decision, and she cannot ultimately be considered responsible. Second, the flower that she flirtatiously throws at a young admirer has been used as evidence of her tampering with men's emotions. However, when he continues to moon over her, it shows that he has lost all sense of proportion about the incident. Third, Laura's oiling of Braggioni's guns has been seen as a masturbatory image indicating that man and woman are basically narcissistic or perverse. Such views only indicate the readers' commitment to intercourse and fear of other types of sexuality.

The story points out that the men who know Laura are disturbed by her virginity, and they wonder why she would support a revolution without a lover involved in it. It is of interest to note that we find some critics following this line of thought to make similar judgments about her. As ⟨Madden⟩ writes: "She rejects sex; she evades love; she substitutes a grim charity; she radiates a deadly innocence." To ask for Laura to have sex with men in this context is equivalent to asking her to be redeemed by men—the very idea against which Porter spoke in her discussion of *Lady Chatterley's Lover*. Although there is evidence in the story that Laura finds it difficult to love, we must resist condemning her for not finding a lover. Laura is described through her clothes as a nunlike figure, but the point we should make is that there is no women's community to give her emotional support. Whereas some nuns have been able to find strength in their women's communities, Laura, the "nun" alone in the world, does not enjoy this option.

—Peter G. Christensen, "Katherine Anne Porter's 'Flowering Judas' and D. H. Lawrence's *The Plumed Serpent:* Contrasting Visions of Women in the Mexican Revolution," *South Atlantic Review* 56, no. 1 (January 1991): pp. 37–38.

NORMAN LAVERS ON LOVE AND BRAGGIONI

[Norman Lavers is a professor of Literature and Creative Writing at Arkansas State University. He has published a novel, a collection of short stories, and critical monographs on Mark Harris, Jerzy Kosinski, and Manuel Puig. In this excerpt, Lavers speaks on the "Courtly Love" tradition carried out by the principal character in the story.]

Braggioni also is dissatisfied. In quite biblical terms he says "It is true everything turns to dust in the hand, to gall on the tongue." "I am disappointed in everything as it comes. Everything. . . . You, poor thing, you will be disappointed too." And finally he tells her, "We are more alike than you realize in some things." She herself thinks, "It may be true I am as corrupt, in another way, as Braggioni . . . as callous, as incomplete."

Incompleteness is the point, and here we see another traditional pattern. The descriptions of Braggioni are all grossly animal: his "Gluttonous bulk," his belt that "creaks like a saddle girth," his eyes that are "the true tawny yellow cat's eyes." He sings in a "furry" voice, "snarling" a tune, and so on. In contradistinction, the descriptions of Laura are so devoid of the animal as to be ethereal: "No dancer dances more beautifully than Laura walks." "She longs to fly out of this room." Laura and Braggioni represent spirit and flesh, the two aspects of being, which need each other for completeness. But to her nun-like spiritual being, the very thought of the flesh (Braggioni) is revolting. Although Braggioni is the symbol of it, symbol of her own animality she has rejected, this rejection makes her reject the flesh in all of its forms: her suitors, and even the innocent children whom she teaches but cannot quite love. Continually we are told of her lack of connection with others. "Nobody touches her." Everyone remains a stranger to her: "The very cells of her flesh reject knowledge and kinship in one monotonous word. No."

West is percipient when he speaks of the three kinds of love: erotic, secular, and divine or Christian. Because he does not recognize the source of these increasingly refined forms of love in the *Symposium* and the Courtly Love tradition, he does not realize they form a sort of progression. But he is exactly right when he says the two poles of the story are the socialist-secular and the Christian-spiritual. I have just suggested that at a deeper level in the symbolical structure, they are body and soul. He is further correct when he says that either one by itself is barren, and only when the two are united by a fructifying love are they vital.

This was Laura's obligation, her role to play in the Courtly Love tradition, to connect the fleshly, through her love, to the spiritual. Braggioni tells Laura of the upcoming May Day disturbances in Morelia: "There will be two independent processions, starting from either end of town [the socialists and the Catholics], and they will march until they meet, and the rest depends. . . ." It depends on Laura to unite these two factions by accepting her own flesh, and by raising the spirituality of her lover by bringing together body and soul. Instead, "Laura holds up the [pistol] belt to him: 'Put that on, and go kill somebody in Morelia, and you will be happier.'" At that very moment Eugenio is dying from the drugs she gave him.

Braggioni now returns to his wife. West says—and in the first part he is correct—that Laura has failed as a complete human being because she has failed at love, whereas Braggioni has succeeded, because he feels pity for his wife, and when she washes his feet there is the suggestion that he is to be interpreted as a Christ-like character, a lover of man. But this scene needs to be looked at more closely, with reference to the Courtly Love Tradition. The scene indeed closely parallels the scene in Luke: "And, behold, a woman in the city, which was a sinner . . . began to wash his feet with tears." But a point has just been made in "Flowering Judas" that his wife is not a sinner: she is perfect and good. When she washes his feet, bathing him with her tears and asking his forgiveness, she is doing what Laura did not do: she is purposely making of him a Christ, a lover of man, raising him up in that way, uniting his flesh with her spirit. Her actions are an example for what Laura's ought to have been.

—Norman Lavers, "'Flowering Judas' and the Failure of *Amour Courtois*," *Studies in Short Fiction* 28, no. 1 (Winter 1991): pp. 80–81.

RAE M. CARLTON COLLEY ON D. H. LAWRENCE AND MEXICO

[Rae M. Carlton Colley has taught English at Emory University. She has published articles on Caroline Lee Hentz and Lydia Maria Child. She has served as editor of *Georgia On My Mind* magazine. In this excerpt, Colley speaks on

Porter's perspective toward Mexico, displayed clearly in the story.]

Although she cultivated a public persona as an elegant Southern belle, Porter actually supported the emancipation of women and believed firmly that women were men's equals in all things. Her Lawrence marginalia confirm this belief. She saw in Lawrence a misogyny that deeply disturbed her and a class-consciousness that damaged his work. Lawrence's characters seemed to consist of lower-class men and the upper-class women to whom they are attracted and whom they try to dominate. This attempt at domination represents a literal manifestation of the patriarchal society Porter so despised. On the surface, Porter and Lawrence seem to be almost polar opposites, so it is no wonder that he held a peculiar fascination for the artistically proper Porter. Lawrence's work, his motives, his vision of truth all seemed muddled to Porter and without substance. Her reviews of both *The Plumed Serpent* and *Lady Chatterley's Lover* (the latter really more a diatribe against censorship than a review) reveal her confusion over Lawrence's use of his undeniable gift for ends that Porter deemed unworthy or, at least, unseemly.

In spite of their surface differences, however, particularly on the subject of sexuality, both writers shared a similar concern with Mexican primitivism that permeates their fiction. Porter disagreed with Lawrence's portrait of the Mexican Indians in *The Plumed Serpent*, calling his novel "a fresh myth of the Indian, a deeply emotional conception, but a myth none the less, and a debased one." However, she admired, almost in spite of herself, Lawrence's eye for detail, his feeling for place, and she noted ⟨in *Collected Essays*⟩ that "a nation-wide political and religious movement provides the framework for a picture that does not omit a leaf, a hanging fruit, an animal, a cloud, a mood, of the visible Mexico." Yet if the "visible" Mexico was accurately and vividly portrayed, the "invisible," mystic Mexico certainly was not. Porter and Lawrence immersed themselves in the political and economic upheaval in revolutionary Mexico, with divergent results. Porter scoffed at Lawrence's fear that while in Mexico he might be murdered. She bragged, "I lived in Mexico then, in Villages and anywhere I wished to go, and never once was threatened. 1920–1925 more or less." Porter overestimates both the duration of her visit and Mexico's safety. In an essay for *Century* magazine, Porter described the growing tide of violence in Mexico: "Uneasiness grows here daily. We are having sudden deportations of foreign agitators, street riots and parades of workers carrying red flags. . . . Battles occur almost daily between Catholics and Socialists in many parts of the Republic." In fact, Porter herself fell under suspicion for her activities, and fearing arrest or deportation, she returned to the United States in 1921.

Porter's several visits to Mexico were inevitably colored by her first glimpse of the country in the 1920s. As a child, her father had whetted her appetite for things Mexican with his enchanting stories, so when the opportunity to travel there on assignments for *Magazine of Mexico* presented itself, Porter eagerly accepted. She arrived in Mexico City just before the inauguration of Álvaro Obregón, whose ascendance to the presidency marked a new era of national optimism for the war-weary Mexican people. Porter threw herself into the causes of the workers with characteristic enthusiasm; she taught Indian children, attended labor union meetings, and took cigarettes and fruit to prisoners of war. She sympathized with the workers who viewed the machine as their salvation, and those pro-socialist convictions found their way into her fiction, especially "Flowering Judas" and the other stories in that collection.

—Rae M. Carlton Colley, "Class and Sexuality in a Mexican Landscape: Katherine Anne Porter's Marginalia on D. H. Lawrence," in *Speaking on the Other Self: American Women Writers*, ed. Jeanne Campbell Reesman (Athens: The University of Georgia Press): pp. 40–41.

JERALDINE KRAVER ON KATHERINE ANNE PORTER AND DIEGO RIVERA

[Jeraldine Kraver is a professor at Michigan State University. Her work has appeared in *Studies in American Jewish Literature* and *LIT*. In this excerpt, Kraver speaks on the relationship between Braggioni, one of the characters in the story, and the painter Diego Rivera.]

While in "The Lovely Legend" Porter questioned Rivera's artistic integrity, in "The Martyr" she indicted his revolutionary commitment. The story opens with the assertion that Ruben is "the most illustrious painter in Mexico." However, he is unable to cope with the defection to a rival artist of his beloved model/mistress Isabel, whose devotion to Ruben was specious at best. Although all of Ruben's friends celebrate the departure of Isabel, noting "he was lucky to lose the lean she-devil," Ruben remains distraught. Her sudden departure leaves him unable to create, and, despite the admonitions of his fellow artists that he must finish his great mural "for the world, for the future," he merely sits before his unfinished work sobbing and growing dangerously fat. Ruben's suffering is maudlin and melodramatic. He laments, "'When she went, she took my life with her . . . my poor little angel Isabel is a murderess, for she has broken my heart.'" After more than six months, his friends quickly tire of his histrionics. Assuaging his sorrow with rich foods and sweet wine, Ruben, a hefty figure to begin with, becomes so obese that he finally collapses and dies over a dish of tamales.

In "The Martyr," Porter suggests that the pathetic figure of Ruben no longer deserves the adulation of those "earnest-minded people" who had "made pilgrimages down the narrow cobbled street, picking their way carefully over puddles in the patio, and clattered up uncertain stairs for a glimpse of the great and yet so simple personage." Ruben is no longer the artist of the revolution. He is duped by Isabel, who stays with him until her lover sells a painting and they can afford to elope. In her farewell note—signed, "Your old friend"—Isabel explains that her new lover "will make a mural with fifty figures of me in it, instead of only twenty." Blinded to the truth of Isabel's character, Ruben continues to worship and idealize her, describing himself as "a martyr to love." In "The Martyr," the ignoble Isabel, not the ideals of the revolution, has become central to Ruben's life and art.

Porter's apparent rejection of Rivera in these two stories clearly corresponds to her disillusionment with the Other she encountered in Mexico, a disillusionment at the core of her most important Mexican story, "Flowering Judas." Indeed, it is no coincidence that the gluttonous Braggioni of "Flowing Judas" looks much like Ruben/Rivera, for Braggioni is as corrupt a revolutionary as Ruben is an artist. Braggioni sings of unrequited love at night in Laura's rooms; Ruben spends his days lamenting his lost love Isabel. In "Flowering Judas," Laura wonders what has happened to the revolution. In "The Martyr," Porter wondered what has happened to the artistic renaissance. What was to have been the symbol of the changes wrought by the Mexican Revolution had become, for Porter, suggestive only of its failures.

—Jeraldine Kraver, "Laughing Best: Competing Correlatives in the Art of Katherine Anne Porter and Diego Rivera," *South Atlantic Review* 63, no. 2 (Spring 1998): pp. 56–57.

Plot Summary of
"Old Mortality"

"Old Mortality" is a short novel set in three parts: "Part I: (1885–1902)," "Part II: 1904," and "Part III: 1912." **Part I** opens with a description of a photograph of Aunt Amy, the legendary family figure who died in her prime. The narrative eye looks out from the perspective of Amy's nieces, Maria and Miranda, who know their aunt "had been beautiful, much loved, unhappy, and she had died young."

When the story begins, Maria and Miranda are twelve and eight years of age, respectively. They have been molded by stories of past generations. Their family, as well as the framework of the story, is built around "a love of legend." Maria and Miranda are influenced not only by the stories they are told, but also by the passion with which their older relatives keep these stories alive.

Though the narrative begins by lumping Maria and Miranda together, the reader is soon made aware of the differences between the two, aside from their varying ages. Miranda, the younger and more imaginative sister, grows up believing that her less flattering features will fade away and she will blossom into a beautiful woman, as her Aunt Amy had. Maria, characterized as the more sensible child, "had no such illusions."

As the story progresses, Porter introduces a number of other family members, many of whom are characterized by their looks and charm—or their lack of such attributes. Cousin Isabel and the "young namesake Amy" are described as graceful dancers and elegant horseback riders, seldom seen without an entourage of young men. Cousin Molly Parrington, though belonging to the generation before Aunt Amy, is "still the belle of the ball." In contrast, her daughter Eva is seen as an ugly old maid. As elaborate as these descriptions get, none live up to Aunt Amy who "belonged to the world of poetry."

Amy's legacy was made even more powerful by her astoundingly meek husband, Uncle Gabriel. After years of unrewarded love, he was finally given the opportunity to marry his beloved Amy, six weeks before her death.

Beyond a love of personal stories, the family holds a great passion for the theater. These outings are always followed by hours of cocktails and critiques: no matter how polished the production, it never measured up to the performances of old. "There was then a life beyond a life in this world, as well as in the next; such episodes confirmed for the little girls the nobility of human feeling, the divinity of man's vision of the unseen, the importance of life and death, the depths of the human heart, the romantic value of tragedy."

The narrative moves from an overview of the family history, largely from Maria and Miranda's perspective, to an account of Uncle Gabriel's state of affairs, as understood by Maria and Miranda. Gabriel makes his living as an owner of race horses and has apparently married an attractive woman, with whom he has a son. Though he has moved on with his life he never gets over the loss of Amy. Every year he sends money for a wreath for her grave, and his words are engraved on her tombstone.

The story moves gracefully from Gabriel's current state to that of his former one, as one of Amy's many suitors. Much of what is known about Aunt Amy comes from stories that the grandmother tells to Cousin Isabel and other members of the family. It is said that Amy's coldness toward Gabriel drove him to drink. She viewed her marriage more like a funeral than a wedding. "If Gabriel praised the frock she was wearing, she was apt to disappear and come back in another."

One of the legendary scandals surrounding Amy's life took place during a Mardi Gras festival. Amy had dressed in a slinky outfit, despite her father's protests, and was escorted to a party by Gabriel. While at the party, she ran into one of her two ex-fiancés, a young Creole gentleman known as Raymond. Much to Gabriel's displeasure, Amy spent most of the evening dancing with him. Toward the end of the night, Gabriel went out to the deck and found Amy and Raymond together. He challenged Raymond to a duel but before they could fight, Harry, Amy's brother (Maria and Miranda's father) shot at the Creole man. It is never entirely clear whether Harry hit the man or not, though after the incident, he moved to Mexico where he stayed until the scandal died down.

Following this incident, Maria and Miranda's great-great-aunt Sally wrote a righteous letter condemning the actions of Amy and

Harry. In this letter she told them to prepare for the worst as they would soon be in God's hands. It was not long before "Great-great-aunt Sally's religious career had become comic legend." She went on to abandon her Catholic ways to marry a Presbyterian man. After finding herself unable to accept the opinions of his faith she "converted to the Hard-Shell Baptists, a sect as loathsome to her husband's family as the Catholic could possibly be." Great-great-aunt Sally "had out-argued, out-fought, and out-lived her entire generation, but she did not miss them. She bedeviled the second generation without ceasing, and was beginning hungrily on the third."

With Harry in exile and Amy actively ignoring her future husband, Gabriel decided to go away. Soon after his departure, following consecutive days of dancing and horse back riding, Amy woke up in a hemorrhage. While she was sick, she began to miss Gabriel and his "sour face." He eventually came back and revealed that his grandfather, who had always considered him the favorite, had, in a distorted state of mind, cut him out of the will.

Part I ends with two letters. The first is from Amy soon after her marriage to Gabriel. In this letter she gives an account of their honeymoon. The next is from Amy's nurse, dated six weeks after the marriage. It says that during the night, Amy consumed an entire bottle of prescription drugs and she had died.

Part II: *1904* opens with a description of the random piece of literature that Maria and Miranda find in their house, "brought in and left there with missionary intent, no doubt, by some Protestant cousin." It is within this literature that they come upon the word "immured" to describe the unlucky maidens, trapped by priests and nuns. They adopt this word and use it to make light of their situation at the Convent of the Child Jesus, in New Orleans, "where they spent the long winters trying to avoid an education." Porter makes it clear that Maria and Miranda have "long since learned to draw the lines between life, which was real and earnest. . . . poetry, which was true but not real. . . . and stories. . . . , in which things happened as nowhere else. . . . (and) there was not a word of truth in them."

When Maria and Miranda perform well in school they are taken to the horse races. One Saturday afternoon, following a good week, their father shows up in the visitor's parlor. He has come from Texas to take them to Crescent City, where Uncle Gabriel is racing a mare.

On the way to the race, the reader is made aware that Miranda has decided to be a jockey, having come to the realization that she will not blossom into a stunning beauty like her deceased Aunt Amy or her cousin Isabel. She decides to keep this a secret, as she wants to surprise her family with the news after she has become an established rider, and she doesn't want her sister Maria to spoil her dreams with dreadful reason.

When they get to the race, Father tells his daughters to place their dollar on Uncle Gabriel's horse, despite the fact that it's a hundred-to-one longshot. Just after they place their bets they run into Uncle Gabriel, who is excited and noticeably intoxicated. Maria and Miranda are particularly surprised by this "vast bulging man with a red face," as they have always heard him described as Aunt Amy's handsome beau. "Oh, what did grown-up people *mean* when they talked, anyway," they wondered.

Uncle Gabriel tells Harry that his daughters are pretty but nothing compared to Amy. He says he named his mare Miss Lucy IV after Amy's old horse, Miss Lucy. Maria lets her uncle know that they have all bet on her.

Everyone is shocked when Miss Lucy wins the race. When they get to the stables they see that Miss Lucy is bleeding badly from the nose and chin, and her legs are trembling. Miranda becomes upset by the sight of the horse. She is ashamed that her joy has to come at such a cost.

Gabriel, who is noticeably drunk at this point, admits that he has not been very successful with his horses. After checking on the condition of Miss Lucy he persuades Harry to bring the girls back to his place to meet his wife, Miss Honey. He tells him that Miss Honey has not been happy for many years; she doesn't like horses and lives entirely for their son Gabe, who has recently moved off to college. He reminisces about Amy's tireless passion for the races.

Gabriel's house is in a poor part of town. Miss Honey is in a perpetual state of gloom. The appearance of Harry and "Amy's nieces," as Gabriel refers to them, does nothing to soften her mood, nor does the news that Miss Lucy has won her race. It does not take long for the tension to mount. Gabriel tries to lighten things up by telling Miss Honey that they can move to a nicer part of town, now that his horse has won. She says she would prefer to stay put rather than move all of her belongings only to move back in three months. Maria and Miranda are shocked that Gabriel and his wife are fighting in front of them. It defies the golden rule that family fights are sacred and should be conducted behind closed doors.

Before Harry and the girls can leave, Miss Honey makes her opinion of her husband's business and his family's affinity for horses evident: "'I had rather, much rather,' said Miss Honey clearly, 'see my son dead at my feet than hanging around a race track.'" When they get back to the car, Maria expresses her relief at finally leaving. In the ensuing silence, Miranda, who had been thinking about her life, says aloud that she's decided against becoming a jockey. Struck by the random nature of her announcement, Maria and Harry start to laugh. Instead of getting upset, Miranda laughs along, lacking the energy to create more tension. **Part II** ends when the girls are dropped off at their school to be "immured" for another week.

Part III: *1912* opens with the narrative eye on Miranda, as she finds her seat in the car of a train. There is an older woman seated across from her whose manner seems cold. After some idle conversation it turns out that the woman is Miranda's cousin, Eva Parrington. Miranda recalls a story of her Aunt Amy threatening to become an old maid like Eva. She remembers that Eva devoted a great deal of time in the effort to earn a woman's right to vote.

Eva speaks to Miranda about the parties she used to attend with Harry and how she had a great deal of fun at those parties despite never finding a husband. Miranda reveals that she hasn't seen her father in over a year. It is at this point that the reader is made aware that they are going home to attend Uncle Gabriel's funeral. Eva comments on Gabriel's "life long infidelity," which will leave his wife Miss Honey resting alone in her grave while Gabriel is buried beside his first wife and his only love.

Eva tells Miranda about the causes she fought for and how she never had success with men. She claims to have always stood up for Aunt Amy, even though she didn't deserve it. She tells of Gabriel's blind devotion to Amy and about Amy's wild ways. This leads her to discuss the scandal that forced Miranda's father into exile. Eva insinuates that Harry had shot the man who attempted to kiss Amy. Miranda responds defensively by saying that her father shot *at* Raymond, but did not hit him. Eva does not confirm nor deny Miranda's statement.

Eva claims that Miranda will understand everything once she's married. Miranda responds, with a certain satisfaction, that she is already married. Eva expresses her disappointment and then changes the focus back to Amy. She believes there is something connected to the scandal with Raymond that led her to marry Gabriel and then led her to death. She believes Amy was trying to avoid some form of disgrace.

As the train ride comes to a close, Eva talks about the insensitive nature of family. She gets emotional as she claims that family members are the first to point out one's weakness, like her weak chin. Miranda takes Eva's hand and helps her to calm down. Eva says she just wanted Miranda to hear another side to the story.

When Eva and Miranda get off the train they are greeted by Harry, who looks noticeably worn down. Miranda gives him a big hug, but he responds with feigned excitement. It is apparent to Miranda that he is still upset about her decision to elope. Harry greets Eva and walks with her to the house.

The narrative meanders through Miranda's thoughts as she walks toward the house. She feels her role within the family changing. She is an adult now, on equal terms with her father and Eva, responsible for her own life and her own mistakes. As the family settles inside, Miranda muses further about the stories she has grown up with and how she is tired of them, how she wants stories of her own. She thinks about how she ran away into marriage to escape her family and how she might run away *from* her marriage. Porter does a skillful job of offering insight into the nature of Miranda's family while not failing to highlight her youth, whimsy, and inexperience. The story ends in the heat of Miranda's thoughts, as she cynically slights the value of love and family and stories when they are substitute for real living. "At least I can know the truth about what happens to me, she assured herself silently, making a promise to herself, in her hopefulness, her ignorance." ❀

List of Characters in
"Old Mortality"

Miranda is one of the principal characters in the story. She is paired with her older sister Maria during the first two parts of the story and then she is the focal point in the third and final part. She is known as the more imaginative and less sensible sister. She elopes when she is eighteen and does not contact her family for over a year. She reunites with everyone at the end of the story for Uncle Gabriel's funeral. Much of the story is told through the eyes, ears, and memory of Miranda and her sister.

Maria is one of the principal characters in the story. She is paired with her younger sister Miranda during the first two parts of the story. She does not appear in the third and final part. She is considered the more sensible sister.

Aunt Amy was a beautiful and legendary figure whose fast life and early death is one of the focal points in the story. She married Gabriel six weeks before she died. She was engaged twice before marrying Gabriel. A scandal with one of her former fiancés forced her brother Harry to live in exile for over a year.

Harry is Amy's brother and Miranda and Maria's father. He is forced into exile after shooting at one of Amy's ex-fiancés. He takes his daughters to see Gabriel's horse race.

Cousin Isabel is one of the beautiful relatives. She is known as a graceful dancer and horseback rider, but not of the caliber of Amy.

Cousin Molly Parrington is Eva's mother. She is known as a charming woman who has been happily widowed twice.

Cousin Eva Parrington is known as Molly's ugly daughter. She never married and spent most of her time trying to earn women's right to vote. She rides the train to Gabriel's funeral with Miranda.

Uncle Gabriel was married to Aunt Amy. He made his living racing horses. After Amy's death he married Miss Honey and had a son. However, he never got over Amy and was buried next to her after his death.

Raymond, a Creole man, was one of Aunt Amy's fiancés prior to Gabriel. Harry was forced into exile after shooting at Raymond.

Miss Honey was Gabriel's second wife. When Maria, Miranda, and Harry met her she was not a happy woman.

Great-great-aunt Sally wrote a righteous letter of warning following Harry's exile to Mexico. ❁

Critical Views on
"Old Mortality"

JANE KRAUSE DEMOUY ON AMY'S BEAUTY

[Jane Krause DeMouy has taught American Literature at the
University of Maryland. Her works include *Katherine Anne
Porter's Women: The Eye of Her Fiction*. In this excerpt,
DeMouy speaks on the memories, details and emotions
contained in the story.]

Similar in structure to "The Old Order," "Old Mortality" is a pastiche
of memories, details, and emotions, "floating ends of narrative"
which Maria and Miranda patch together as well as they can, the
"fragments of tales that were like bits of poetry or music. . . ." And
like the memories of the Old Order, they have been "packed away
and forgotten for a great many years." It is ostensibly Amy's story,
told from a number of points of view, but all is sifted through
Miranda's perception. In actuality, the chronology of the story
belongs to Miranda, and the tale depends primarily on what she will
do with the legend of Amy and the bitter reality of Cousin Eva.

If "The Old Order" is a catalogue of the "giants" of Miranda's
childhood who taught her what a woman might be, "Old Mortality"
is the story of Miranda's confrontation with the most formidable
archetype her society can offer: the Southern belle, a nineteenth-
century American manifestation of the virgin love goddess.

Obviously, Amy was once a person who has now become a legend;
she was "beautiful, much loved, unhappy, and she . . . died young."
The mystery in her behavior encourages others to speculate aloud
about her and the meaning of her actions. Enigmatic, devilish, mag-
netic to men, she has also been capricious, toying with Gabriel's
affection, agreeing to marry two other men, and then subsequently
breaking those engagements without reason. She has been the cause
of a near duel and her brother Harry's flight to Mexico; and yet she
never offers an explanation of the affair. Finally, after dismissing
Gabriel summarily, she whimsically agrees to marry him when he is
disinherited. Her family says good-bye to her after her wedding, and
six weeks later she is dead, perhaps by suicide.

A more romantic and tragic combination of circumstances is not to be imagined, conjuring as they do the likes of Juliet, Madame Bovary, and Anna Karenina. Then too, Amy is a dark lady—not only Shakespeare's, but Hawthorne's, and certainly Poe's—with more sensuousness and dangerous allure than virginity would ordinarily allow.

Amy's physical beauty supposedly corresponds in every detail to her family's standard of female perfection:

> First, a beauty must be tall; whatever color the eyes, the hair must be dark, the darker the better; the skin must be pale and smooth. Lightness and swiftness of movement were important points. A beauty must be a good dancer, superb on horseback, with a serene manner, an amiable gaiety tempered with dignity at all hours. Beautiful teeth and hands, of course, and over and above all this, some mysterious crown of enchantment that attracted and held the heart.

But it is interesting that Miranda, studying the old-fashioned portrait of Amy with her cropped hair and "reckless smile," is left wondering what was so enticing about this compelling girl, about whom everything and nothing was known. The obvious implication is that Amy was in reality a young woman whose graces and physical charms have been exaggerated by the family, who take more pleasure in the reflected glory they receive from their relationship to this angelic mystery than they do in the accuracy of their descriptions. There is undoubtedly some of that, but there is also the persistent fact that Amy really was a charmer, with at least two other suitors who wanted to marry her. There is something more to Amy's dark beauty than an appealing prettiness. A less romantic generation would reject the term "crown of enchantment" and call it sex appeal, but it is not quite the simple matter Cousin Eva makes it, either, when she describes Victorian mating rituals as "just sex." Amy's allure is rather a complex combination of sublimated sexual energy, real allure, and personal restraint.

—Jane Krause DeMouy, *Katherine Anne Porter's Women: The Eye of Her Fiction* (Austin: University of Texas Press, 1979): pp. 146–48.

[Darlene Harbour Unrue is a professor of English at the University of Nevada, Las Vegas. Her works include *Truth and Vision in Katherine Anne Porter's Fiction* and *Understanding Katherine Anne Porter*. In this excerpt, Unrue discusses the romantic ideals contained in the story.]

"Old Mortality" also revolves around romantic ideals, romantic love and the past. The ideal of romantic love is embodied in the love story of Amy and Gabriel, told in part 1: 1885–1902. The story centers on the beautiful Amy, who died young, and the somber, tenacious Gabriel, who had everything, "youth, health, good looks, the prospect of riches, . . . a devoted family circle," and after five years, Amy herself. The Amy legend was based on a Porter family legend, the unhappy story of Annie and Thomas Gay. It probably also incorporated Porter's idealistic view of her own mother, a view created by her father's sentimental and guilt-ridden recollections of his wife.

The viewpoint of the first part is that of the little girls Miranda and Maria, and their perception of romantic love is analyzed in an irony that contrasts an implied truth with what the little girls believe to be truth. The romantic ideal is fostered by their elders, and they accept their elders' assertions even in the face of conflicting evidence. Miranda and Maria are disturbed by the "evidence"—"the visible remains"—but trust the "truth" that exists in the memory of the elders. Even though Amy of the photograph has a "reckless indifferent smile" and her clothes are "terribly out of fashion," they believe their father, who says of the photograph, "It's not very good. Her hair and her smile were her chief beauties, and they are not shown at all." And they believe their Uncle Bill, who answers their "Was she really beautiful?" with "As an angel, my child."

Amy has been idealized as the beautiful, unapproachable woman of chivalric tradition—idolized by the dashing and patient suitor in the person of Gabriel. The legend does not pretend that Amy herself had romantic notions about love and marriage; it admits indeed to Amy's having not loved Gabriel at all. But the Gabriel of memory is fully developed in the ideal of romantic love. Even his tendency toward profligacy, apparent early on, is explained as the result of Amy's coldness to him. Ostensibly he suffers Amy's rejection for five years, plies her with extravagant gifts from caged lovebirds to enameled flowers, endures jealousies, challenges a rival to a duel, and goes forth to exile until Amy changes her mind and agrees to marry him. She dies six weeks after the marriage, and in their minds' eyes the little girls see Gabriel suffering from a broken heart through the long years after. Once he wrote a poem about Amy, had it printed in gold on a mourning card, and sent it to a great many members of the family.

Thus Miranda and Maria's romantic ideal is centered in Uncle Gabriel, whose name identifies him as a celestial being; the ideal is amplified by their adolescent reading of sentimental and Gothic romances in which virtuous and beautiful heroines are immured in convents by villainous religiouses. The girls, who attend the school of the Convent of the Child Jesus, identify with the "unlucky" immured maidens of their forbidden reading matter. Their awakening and the concurrent disillusionment occur when Miranda and Maria are "freed" from the convent for a Saturday outing with their father, who comes to take them to the horse races, where their Uncle Gabriel, whom they never have seen, is running a horse. The release from the convent will be more than a day of freedom from the school's restrictive rules; the girls also will be released from their false notions about Uncle Gabriel and about love itself.

—Darlene Harbour Unrue, *Truth and Vision in Katherine Anne Porter's Fiction* (Athens: The University of Georgia Press, 1985): pp. 124–26.

GEORGE HENDRICK AND WILLENE HENDRICK ON FAMILY LEGENDS

[George Hendrick is a professor of English at the University of Illinois at Urbana-Champaign. He is the author of numerous articles on American literary figures, among them Washington Irving, Ralph Waldo Emerson, Henry David Thoreau, Walt Whitman, and Tennessee Williams. Willene Lowery Hendrick coedited with George Hendrick *On the Illinois Frontier: Dr. Hiram Rutherford, 1840–1848*. In this excerpt, Willene and George Hendrick speak on Porter's use of personal family legends as a model for the story.]

In her biography of Porter Joan Givner has shown that Porter incorporated into her family legend stories she had heard recounted by her Aunt Ione, wife of Harrison's younger brother. Ione had been educated in a New Orleans convent. She had beautiful clothes and jewels; she had lived a life quite different from that of the Porters in their cramped four-room house in Kyle, and she was idolized by the young Callie. Givner has also shown that when Porter went to Bermuda in 1929 she lived for a time at Hilgrove, the kind of spacious mansion in which she would like to have been born. She incorporated the fine old china, the furnishings, and the library of Hilgrove into her fictional past.

Porter's short novel begins on a note of ironic contrast between beauty and impermanence. Both Miranda and Maria hear adults say, "How lovely," on seeing the photograph of Amy, who is now dead. True, her picture shows a spirited-looking woman, but she is caught in the "pose of being photographed, a motionless image in her dark walnut frame." The background of the picture seems faded and Amy's costume appears old-fashioned, like the finery much loved by Grandmother Rhea.

In "Part I (1885–1902)," the children hear the family legends about Amy (literally, "the beloved"), and while the children are observant enough to see that some details of the legend are untrue, they go on believing in them. The naive Miranda even believes that Mary, Queen of Scots, died on stage the night of the performance. Obviously, then, Miranda could believe that romantically consumptive Amy would toy with Gabriel's affections, would inspire men to fight over her, would copy her Mardi Gras ball dress from the Dresden china shepherdess in the parlor. The grandfather, returned from the grave for this story, orders Amy to make her costume more respectable, but Amy argues that he had been looking at the Dresden shepherdess for years without objection. To Mr. Rhea, however, art and life are different. Amy obeys but appears at the party dressed even more daringly.

Gabriel, Harry, and Mariana, Harry's fiancé and (and perhaps a romantic rendering of Harrison Porter's wife, Mary Alice), all watch Amy's behavior with some dismay as young men, some of rather dubious character, flock about her. Later that night a former suitor named Raymond and dressed as Jean Lafitte arrives, goes onto the gallery with Amy, and according to family legend may have kissed her, whereupon Gabriel challenges the pirate to a duel and Harry defends Amy's honor by shooting at Raymond. The legend goes on and on with the events taking on the overtones of a romantic Southern novel: Harry's flight to Mexico, Amy's dramatic ride with him to the border, Gabriel sent away and disinherited, the wedding of Gabriel and Amy, their honeymoon in New Orleans, and finally Amy's death six weeks after the wedding.

These stock scenes, presented to the children as reality, are challenged in parts II and III. Part II, set in 1904 after the death of the grandmother and after the children have been sent to a convent school, begins by contrasting the sedate, dull convent lives the girls live with the anti-Catholic stories the girls have read about nuns immured in convents and killing their babies. The girls have to give up trying to fit those violent stories to their life. They are indeed "immured" in the convent, but not in the sense meant in the trashy novels they read in the summer. Being "immured" gives a feeling of glamor to their dull, sterile lives. They are "hedged and confined," isolated in their muslin-curtained cells at night (just as Stephen is confined in *A Portrait of the Artist as a Young Man*), cut off from the outside world except on Saturday afternoons when they are allowed, if they have not broken too many regulations, to attend the races.

—Willene Hendrick and George Hendrick, *Katherine Anne Porter* (Boston: Twayne Publishers, 1988): pp. 55–57.

Darlene Harbour Unrue on Porter's Sources and Influences

[Darlene Harbour Unrue is a professor of English at the University of Nevada, Las Vegas. Her works works include *Truth and Vision in Katherine Anne Porter's Fiction* and *Understanding Katherine Anne Porter*. In this excerpt, Unrue speaks on the literary influences that manifest in the story.]

All this is not to say that Porter was never inspired by another work or another writer or indeed that she never borrowed from them.

There surely are echoes of Henry James, Austen, Flaubert, and Joyce, among others, in Porter's fiction. For example, the creation of the child Miranda in "The Circus," "The Fig Tree," "The Grave," and "Old Mortality" probably was inspired in part by the child characters of Henry James, as was Stephen in "The Downward Path to Wisdom." Porter, who admired finely drawn child characters, said that James' children were the best in all of fiction and praised his understanding of the child as a stranger in an adult world. Many critics also have noted the similarity between Porter's style and Austen's, centered in their technical habits of placing rich meanings in restrained language. A strong case can also be made for the influence on Porter of Homer's *Odyssey* and Dante's *Divine Comedy*. Porter consistently named Homer and Dante among the greatest of artists. In "A Defense of Circe" (1954), Porter called the *Odyssey* "the most enchanting thing ever dreamed of in the human imagination." In 1963 she told Caroline Gordon that she considered the *Odyssey* the "greatest single piece of literature in all history." She wrote to Eugene Pressly in 1932 that she was working on "that book of Amy" (obviously "Old Mortality") and that she had named the second of its three parts "Midway of this Mortal Life," a translation of the first line from Dante's *Inferno*. Her broad theme of rite of passage and her pervasive canonical metaphors of the journey and of descent into hell and ascent to enlightenment may well have been inspired by the *Odyssey* and *Divine Comedy*. However, the unavailability of definitive proof suggests that Porter assimilated her influences so perfectly, as Hartley observed early on, that even her literary sources became her personal experience.

Porter's assimilation of her sources made it possible for her to meet her own literary standards. She consistently described truth-telling as a literary technique rather than simply a moral standard, and she repeatedly praised careful craftsmanship. She said that her one aim was to tell a straight story and to give true testimony. The agent of that aim was precise language that refused embellishment and contrivance. For Porter, the artist was not prophet, reformer, or politician. "It is not the artist's business," she wrote Bill Hale in 1932, "to divine the future, unless he has the faculty of divination and happens also to be an artist." Describing the artist as "sublimely superfluous," she said that artists' work is rediscovered when people want a "fuller record of the past" or when they want "light on the present predicament," but sometimes only when they want a work that is "fresh and beautiful and new." She divided artists into two camps, which she called the James-minded people and the Whitman-minded people, and declared that she herself was firmly on the side of James. M. M. Liberman points out that in James, Porter obviously saw the triumph of "making"—the effective ordering of experience by means of style.

—Darlene Harbour Unrue, "Porter's Sources and Influences," in *Katherine Anne Porter and Texas: an Uneasy relationship,* eds. Clinton Machann and William Bedford Clark (College Station: Texas A&M University Press): pp. 105–7.

Janis P. Stout on the Expectations in the Story

[Janis P. Stout is a professor of English at Texas A&M University. Her works include the novels *Home Truth, Eighteen Holes,* and *A Family Likeness.* In this excerpt, Stout speaks on the feminine independence contained in the story.]

"Old Mortality," first published in 1937 in the *Southern Review,* has often been considered Porter's finest work. It was recognized by Cleanth Brooks and Robert Penn Warren with inclusion in their enormously influential 1943 anthology, *Understanding Fiction,* a watershed of the New Criticism, and it has been included in numerous other anthologies for college students. Warren believed the story had "few peers in any language." In many ways, it stands as the summing up of Porter's creative impulse. Its theme, the struggle toward self-definition, is the central theme of her own life. Thus it can properly be read as a pervasively autobiographical work, though not directly autobiographical in the way that it has sometimes been seen. Details of setting and family circumstance, with their trappings of prosperity and social prominence, convey more of wish than of actual remembrance. Indeed, as George Core has commented in reference to the "Old Order" stories, the surface of the story "often parallels her invented life" more than her actual one. But the deeply embedded thematic action of "Old Mortality," a struggle toward self-definition through acts of separation from family and home, is profoundly self-revelatory. Journeys and displacements were primal symbolic actions in Porter's own developing awareness of self, as they are in Miranda's.

The story follows Miranda's development of a mental independence that will allow her to launch her adult life. She does this largely through studying the important women of her family, past and present, and observing the unreasonable, contradictory responses that these women evoke on the part of fathers, brothers, lovers, and husbands, as well as on the part of the powerful grandmother figure. In particular, she is tormented by the family's idealizing of her deceased Aunt Amy, now "only a ghost in a frame" but still held up to Miranda and her sister as a seemingly impossible ideal of feminine beauty and charm, the "quintessential belle." Besides their family's Amy-olatry, the two girls also puzzle over their father's stubborn denial of the truth about other women in the family. He insists, for example, that "there were never any fat women in the family" despite the plain fact that at least two of their great-aunts are quite obese. Clearly, everyone in the family values slenderness, gracefulness, charm. Their father, who values these qualities to the point of refusing to recognize any departure from them, not only sets the girls an impossible standard of female perfection but makes his love contingent on their approximating these standards. Like Porter's own father, he doles out affection on the basis of their being "prettily dressed and well behaved, and pushed them away if they had not freshly combed hair and nicely scrubbed fingernails."

Porter makes it clear that such demanding models of feminine perfection exert a destructive pressure on those female children and young women who cannot attain them. Not only does Miranda live in continual torment because of her fear that she cannot be another Amy, she learns, late in the story, how cruelly the judging of young women by their beauty alone has blighted the life of her cousin Eva, who lost out to other girls in the vicious contest for husbands simply because she had no chin and therefore could not present herself as a belle. Eva has found her own satisfactions in a career as teacher and crusader for woman suffrage. Even so, she bears emotional scars that are all too evident, and she is depicted in a "stereotypical way" that has been seen as reflecting Porter's ambivalence toward feminists.

In the final section of the story, as Miranda takes a train home for a family funeral along with Cousin Eva, she hears Eva's assault on the family legend of the beautiful Amy. Readers sometimes interpret this assault as a correction of fantasy by fact, but Eva simply replaces the legend of the belle with her own legend, equally overdramatized, of the "impure woman." Listening to her diatribe, Miranda realizes that Cousin Eva hates Amy, dead though she is, but she is not yet sufficiently free of the myth of beautiful womanhood to understand why. What Eva hates is actually the image of the belle which, held up as an impossible yardstick against which she had to measure herself, has left her frustrated and emotionally twisted.

The real Amy, hidden behind the family's idealization, is revealed by Porter in a few deft strokes. The Amy that the family refuses to recognize and Eva cannot recognize because she is blinded by resentment is herself a frustrated model of self-definition through disaffection. Self-willed, defiant of convention, she plays out the expected role of belle and bride in her own style. When she marries she refuses to wear the white dress symbolizing values of propriety and stability, but instead chooses a gray dress accessorized with red, the color of blood, telling her mother "'I shall wear mourning if I like . . . it is *my* funeral, you know.'" She is remembered in family lore in her moment of departure after the wedding as she "ran into the gray cold and stepped into the carriage and turned and smiled with her face as pale as death." Even without the comment that "none of us saw her alive again," it is quite clear that hers is an ultimate departure. But in the family legend her bold gestures are remembered as evidence of her flamboyant nature, not as a substantive protest. Only the attentive reader sees that she has enacted a parody of the feminine ideal.

—Janis P. Stout, *Katherine Anne Porter: A Sense of the Times* (Charlottesville: University of Virginia Press, 1995): pp. 192–94.

M. K. FORNATARO-NEIL ON THE FAMILY LEGENDS

[M. K. Fornataro-Neil received a graduate degree in Literature at Indiana University of Pennsylvania. In this excerpt, Fornataro-Neil speaks on the structure of the story.]

In "Old Mortality," perhaps the most complex variation of this paradigm, Porter directs the reader to recognize the narrative construct written by the elder members of Miranda's family. Frequent and repeated use of the words *story, legend, narrative,* and *tale* underscores the fictive nature of the family's reconstruction of the past. In essence, Miranda's family has constructed a highly romanticized narrative about the past that depends greatly on the story of Amy. Because Amy, in some external ways, conforms to the ideals of the southern belle of the Old South, she becomes a central and defining element. Although her own personal reality is quite different from the way she is defined by the family, Amy becomes emblematic of the romantic ideal.

As Jane Krause DeMouy notes, "'Old Mortality' is a fiction of memory. . . ." It is significant that Porter never writes from the perspective of the past, from the time that Amy actually lives and dies. Rather, Amy is presented to the reader through a continual writing (and rewriting) of history, based on the memories of those who knew her. Because her life is reconstructed by others, Amy never really has a chance to speak for herself, to Miranda or Maria or to the reader; she is, essentially, a silent figure. Aunt Amy is "only a ghost in a frame, and a sad, pretty story from old times." The girls must sort through the pieces of Amy's story they are given, as well as the preserved physical evidence (Amy's photograph, wedding dress, etc.), in order to construct their own narratives, their own interpretations of the story, and to come to some understanding of Amy's identity:

> They listened, all ears and eager minds, picking here and there among the floating ends of narrative, patching together as well as they could fragments of tales that were like bits of poetry or music, indeed were associated with the poetry they had heard or read, with music, with the theater.

Furthermore, it is clear that even within this narrative, the carefully constructed illusion of her family's memory, Amy seems to speak a different language, one that her family is incapable of understanding. Operating as she did outside the societal conventions of her time, Amy's sign system differed radically from that of her family and community. Not only does Amy reject a white gown for her wedding, she redefines the word *wedding* as being synonymous with the word *funeral.* For her, marriage does not mean a cure for her illness, as her mother has assured her. Rather, it means death. She tells here mother, "It is *my* funeral, you know." Amy's mother (Miranda's grandmother) makes little, if any, attempt to interpret Amy's language or to recognize her daughter's unsuitability for the life imposed on her. To do so would upset the family's narrative, which relies on Amy as the symbol of ideal womanhood. Amy too seems to realize her role within the narrative, to sense that she is a "written" character. At one point she says, "And if I am to be the heroine of this novel, why shouldn't I make the most of it?"

Since Amy was apparently neither as beautiful as she is remembered to be, nor as virtuous, just how is it that she represents the southern belle, the southern ideal? As DeMouy has pointed out, the view of Amy as southern belle, despite her failure to live up to the ideal, is largely dependent on the presence of the ardent suitor, Gabriel. While the defining character of the narrative is Amy, the so-called romance between Amy and Gabriel becomes the central myth, the legend that sustains Amy's role.

Both Amy and Gabriel have, in effect, been written by others so as to conform to the romantic ideal of the Old South. Gabriel is written as "a handsome and romantic young man" who has everything, including "youth, health, good looks, the prospect of riches, and a devoted family circle." But Gabriel is not exactly the picture-perfect suitor for Amy. Her longstanding refusal to marry him is said to have "driven Gabriel to a wild life and even to drinking." What's more, Gabriel's use of horse racing as a means to make a living, rather than as an idle pastime, is not considered to be gentlemanly and results in his being cut off from the family fortune. It is only Gabriel's worship of Amy that enables Miranda's family to write his identity to suit their narrative. When Miranda and Maria at last have a chance to see their renowned Uncle Gabriel, they are shocked that this huge, shabby, blustering drunkard could possible be the hero of their parents' stories. The disenchanting sight of Gabriel leads them to further question the already suspect narrative they have heard:

> "Can that be our Uncle Gabriel?" their eyes asked. "Is that Aunt Amy's handsome romantic beau? Is that the man who wrote the poem about our Aunt Amy?" Oh, what did grown-up people *mean* when they talked, anyway?

Ironically, after Gabriel's death, Eva Parrington and Miranda's father express sympathy for him, but still miss the tragic reality of his hopeless and desperate adoration of an impossible ideal. Miranda's father says, "Life for Gabriel . . . was just one perpetual picnic."

—M. K. Fornataro-Neil, "Constructed Narratives and Writing Identity in the Fiction of Katherine Anne Porter," *Twentieth Century Literature* 44, no. 3 (Fall 1998): pp. 349–51.

Plot Summary of
"Pale Horse, Pale Rider"

"Pale Horse, Pale Rider," the title piece from Porter's collection of three short novels, opens with an abstract description, drifting between first and third person narration, of a disoriented female character who is unsure whose bed she is rising from and which horse she should take on her journey past "Death and the Devil." She decides on Graylie and rides off beside someone referred to as "the stranger." It is quickly apparent that "the stranger" is familiar to her. She forces Graylie to stop and watches as he rides past.

The narrative takes more concrete form once the female character is identified as Miranda. She forces herself to wake from the depths of this dream and waits "in a daze for life to begin again." This dream-like opening is called back into play toward the end of the story as Miranda, who is taken ill, wakes inside the hospital after months of battling influenza.

The story grounds itself inside a small-town newspaper office where Miranda works as a theater critic. Two men are sitting on her desk when she arrives. They are government officials who interrogate her for neglecting to purchase a fifty dollar Liberty Bond. She tells them she only makes eighteen dollars a week and she can not afford to invest. They claim she's the only person in the office who has not invested and that it could prove dangerous to her if she continues to withhold her money.

As the two men leave, the narrative moves ahead one day, after Miranda has woken up. She thinks about her friend Mary Townsend, the society editor, whom everyone calls Towney. Towney and Miranda both held "real" reporting jobs until their morals prevented them from exploiting a victim of abuse. When the rival paper printed the story, they were demoted and given "female jobs," writing on society and theater. It turns out that Towney has also failed to invest in a Liberty Bond. She claims that Bill, the city editor, would never fire them for failing to invest.

Miranda and Towney decide to accompany a group of women who are going to the hospitals to do charitable deeds for the servicemen. Miranda walks around with a basket of goods and approaches a man with a particularly hostile expression. When he refuses to take anything from her she leaves the hospital and is overcome with anxiety.

Miranda tries to counter her anxiety by thinking about happier times; events that took place the previous night, when she danced with a lieutenant named Adam who resides in the same boarding house. On her way home from the hospital, she runs into him in the hallway. He tells her that he doesn't have to go back to camp quite yet and they will be able to spend more time together.

Adam is twenty-four years old and a second lieutenant in a corps of engineers. He is on leave but expects to be sent overseas any day. Miranda is also twenty-four and it is clear, even though they've only known each other for ten days, that their characters are very compatible. It is also clear that they both have felt the pressures of war.

After heading outside to take a walk, Adam mentions the mysterious plague that has killed several soldiers and others that have come in contact with them. As they talk, a funeral procession passes them by. They walk into a restaurant for a late night meal and Miranda reveals that she is not feeling well, but refrains from dwelling on her condition. Upon returning from the restaurant she feels a wave of sadness come over her. She likes Adam but fears he is destined to die in the war.

The narrative resumes back in the newspaper office where Towney and Chuck Rouncivale, the sports reporter, are sitting at Miranda's desk. As they talk, Miranda's mind wanders on to Adam. The short time they have spent together in restaurants, walking the streets and in the mountains, and visiting museums and theater houses has had a profound effect on her. She gets lost in her thoughts until the sound of Bill shouting at someone in the office breaks her out of her meandering mind.

The reader is made aware that Chuck has talked to Miranda about his preference for theater writing over sports. He can't understand why women are always given the theater jobs and men the sports. As Miranda gets set to leave the office, she is confronted by a small man whose play had been panned in the paper. He claims that other publications have praised his work and he demands to know why Miranda trashed it. He gets increasingly worked up until Chuck intervenes and escorts Miranda out of the office. Following this incident, Miranda is shaken up and outwardly depressed. She feels the weight of everything around her closing in. Chuck claims that she makes things difficult on herself by refusing to play the game. He says that if she learns who to please she won't have to worry so much.

Miranda and Chuck attend a play which turns out to be dreadful. Chuck rants about what he'd write if he were the drama critic. She tells him that she's going away soon and encourages him to write the review in her place. She senses that something terrible is beginning to happen to her. In addition to the stress she feels over Adam's imminent departure, she suspects that her health is on the decline.

The narrative moves to another encounter with Adam, as he and Miranda sit through a dreary play relating to the war. Miranda tells Adam that she feels the "'worst of war is the fear and suspicion and the awful expression in all the eyes you meet.'" She goes on to say that she too lives in fear and that nobody should have to live in that state. "'It's what war does to the mind and the heart, Adam, and you can't separate these two—what it does to them is worse than what it can do to the body.'" Adam responds by saying that if he didn't go, he wouldn't be able to live with himself. Miranda thinks of him as a sacrificial lamb.

After Miranda writes a review of the dreary play, she and Adam go to a social establishment to drink and dance. Despite her failing health and her anxiety over Adam's inevitable departure, Miranda has an enjoyable time.

The narrative resumes the following evening. Miranda has just woken out of a deep sleep. She is not well. Adam enters her room and claims that he had been held up at camp. He says that Miss Hobbes, who works in the boarding house where they both reside, told him that Miranda was ill. Adam finds a prescription that the doctor had left for Miranda and he goes off to a drugstore to get it filled.

While Adam is gone, Miranda's mind runs through images and thoughts of her past and present. She falls asleep again and wakes by the sound of her own voice, screaming about the horrors of war. Miss Hobbes and Adam are at the door. Miss Hobbes demands that

Adam take Miranda out of the boarding house as it is obvious that she is afflicted with the plague. He assures her that she will be out by morning and that he will take care of her. Adam tells Miranda that the entire town has been devastated by the plague and that most of the stores and restaurants are closed.

Miranda takes her medicine and immediately vomits it up. Adam calls one of the hospitals to plead for a room but he is denied. They start a conversation about life and their pasts and how precious even the unhappy times seem to them now. They recognize that they are both facing death, Adam with the war and Miranda with her illness. In the effort to keep Miranda awake, they decide to recite all the prayers and spiritual songs they can remember. It is here that the title of the story comes into play, as they try to remember the lines that make up the spiritual "Pale Horse, Pale Rider." The song is about the many things that the rider has taken away. Miranda mentions that "'Death always leaves one singer to mourn.'" As Miranda starts to fall back to sleep, she confesses that she's in love with Adam. Just before she trails off, Adam admits that he's also in love with her.

The narrative tracks the obscure events of Miranda's dream until she wakes, presumably the following day, and tries to describe her dream to Adam. He listens politely and then goes out to get some ice cream and coffee. While he's gone, two interns from the County Hospital arrive to take Miranda to the hospital. They had responded to the aggressive pressure put on them from Bill, the city editor. While the interns carry Miranda to the ambulance she expresses concern for Adam. The interns assure her that they will leave a note for him.

The story continues at the hospital where Miranda is steadily losing her grasp on reality. She has identified with Dr. Hildesheim, who tells her that Adam has visited a few times and will be back. A nurse named Miss Tanner has a note from him. Miranda is not capable of reading it on her own so Miss Tanner reads it to her. The note says that Adam has not been allowed to see her, though he will continue to try. When Miss Tanner leaves, Miranda can not remember what had been read.

The narrative takes on the form of Miranda's dreamlike consciousness. Through abstract description, the reader is made aware of movement in the hospital and the fact that people are dying.

Miranda is looked after by Dr. Hildesheim and Miss Tanner. She is "no longer aware of the members of her own body, entirely withdrawn from all human concerns, yet alive with a peculiar lucidity and coherence. . . . composed entirely of one single motive, the stubborn will to live."

Miranda emerges from the throes of her illness after the war has ended. Chuck Rouncivale and Towney come to see her, carrying letters that had accumulated while she was incoherent. She expresses her delight in finding herself alive. Miss Tanner encourages her to read her letters. Most of them are from friends wishing her well, except one, in unfamiliar handwriting, from a soldier in Adam's camp. The letter says that Adam died from influenza at the camp hospital. Chuck and Towney make arrangements to help Miranda get back on her feet. The story ends as she pays her final respects to Adam, for whom she claims to have survived. ❀

List of Characters in
"Pale Horse, Pale Rider"

Miranda is the principal character in the story. She works as a theater critic for a small town newspaper. She contracts influenza and spends a large portion of the story in the hospital. She falls in love with Adam, a second lieutenant in a unit of engineers who gets called off to war and dies of influenza in the camp hospital.

Adam is a second lieutenant in an engineering corps. He falls in love with Miranda and spends his entire leave with her. He gets called off to fight and dies of influenza in the camp hospital.

Mary (Towney) Townsend is Miranda's closest female friend. She works as the society editor for the same newspaper as Miranda.

Bill is the city editor for Miranda's paper. He is able to get Miranda a hospital room after she becomes ill.

Chuck Rouncivale is the sports reporter for the newspaper. He attends a theater performance with Miranda and confesses that he would prefer to write theater reviews rather than sports columns.

Miss Hobbe works at the boarding house where Miranda and Adam meet. She tries to kick Miranda out of her room when she falls ill.

Dr. Hildesheim is the hospital doctor who takes care of Miranda.

Miss Tanner is the hospital nurse who looks after Miranda. She encourages her to read her letters once she is recovered. ❀

Critical Views on
"Pale Horse, Pale Rider"

DARLENE HARBOUR UNRUE ON MIRANDA'S DREAM

[Darlene Harbour Unrue is a professor of English at the University of Nevada, Las Vegas. Her works works include *Truth and Vision in Katherine Anne Porter's Fiction* and *Understanding Katherine Anne Porter.* In this excerpt, Unrue speaks on the dream-like opening in the story.]

"Pale Horse, Pale Rider" is written in a structured stream-of-consciousness form with Porter guiding the reader through Miranda's dreams and describing the action that holds the dreams together in a plot. The story falls into three parts, like a play, with the first part introducing Miranda and extending to her the collapse from illness. The most panoramic of the units, it depicts Miranda as a social being, the scenes shifting from her room to the newspaper office to the theatre, the dance hall, and the streets of the city. The second part describes Miranda's night of delirium in the room of the boardinghouse, with Miranda and Adam in the forestage. The third section reveals Miranda alone in the hospital, with only minor characters in the background, and it ends with her reentry into the world. Dispersed among the three units are five dreams, the interpretations of which are critical to understanding all the meanings of the story.

The dream, vision, or reverie is a particular form that Porter favored throughout her writing. In her introduction to Eudora Welty's *A Curtain of Green* she admits to a "deeply personal preference" for the kind of story in which "external act and the internal voiceless life of the human imagination almost meet and mingle on the mysterious threshold between dream and waking, one reality refusing to admit or confirm the existence of the other, yet both conspiring toward the same end." "Pale Horse, Pale Rider" is such a story. It is a combination of the waking life of Miranda and the sleeping reality in which truth is revealed to her in ways it could not otherwise be revealed.

The opening dream, the only one in the first section, sets into motion the most important symbols and establishes the ironic pattern and the major themes of the story. It displays Miranda's early struggle to assert her identity within her family (a link to "Old Mortality"), her fear of engulfment by her family, and her emerging awareness of death. The color gray (or silver) is prominent, as the middle ground between black and white (symbolizing interchangeably life and death), in the name of Miranda's horse "Graylie," who is not afraid of bridges, in the color of the stranger's horse, and in the memory of her kitten. The stranger, who is Death, is vaguely familiar to Miranda ("I know this man if I could place him. He is no stranger to me"), an acquaintanceship that is reminiscent of Porter's comment that "We are born knowing death." A symbolic journey also is begun in this section, but Miranda "does not mean to take it" (her dying is premature at this point) and wakes before it is completed. She wakes to the word "war," which is also a gong of warning. The remainder of the long first section develops the ideas of death, war, and journey, as Miranda's waking world and her social context are described.

—Darlene Harbour Unrue, *Understanding Katherine Anne Porter* (Columbia: University of South Carolina Press, 1988): pp. 105–7.

George Cheatham on Death in Porter's Stories

[George Cheatham is a professor of English at Eastern Kentucky University. He has published articles on a variety of authors, including Shakespeare, Keats, Byron, Conrad, Hemingway, Faulkner, and O'Connor. In this excerpt, Cheatham speaks on what remains for Miranda at the end of the story.]

Gone for Miranda is the old order, the old painful structure; gone are the Judeo-Christian conceptions of life, death, and afterlife contained, for example, in Uncle Gabriel's poem for Amy's tombstone:

> She lives again who suffered life,
> Then suffered death, and now set free

A singing angel, she forgets
The griefs of old mortality.

What remains for Miranda, what she chooses to retain, is only the griefs of old mortality—that is, the freedom of the unconnected present, the here and now of her own experience, of herself and her own world, apparently including death:

> Ah, but there is my own life to come yet, she thought, my own life now and beyond. I don't want any promises, I won't have any false hopes, I won't be romantic about myself. I can't live in their world any longer, she told herself, listening to the voices [of her father and Aunt Eva]. Let them tell their stories to each other. Let them go on explaining how things happened. I don't care. At least I can know the truth about what happens to me, she assured herself silently, making a promise to herself, in her hopefulness, her ignorance.

Here in "Old Mortality," Miranda's choice, in this promise to herself, of the personal over the mythic parallels her earlier choice in the first part of "The Grave." The consequence of this choice as well generally repeats "The Grave." For in "Pale Horse, Pale Rider" as earlier, the initial gaiety of her choice turns, ultimately, to despair, as the implicit "ignorance" of that choice becomes manifest. Miranda may dream of a beautiful, sufficient "nothing," but she must awaken each day to face modernity's inescapably nightmarish aspects.

Detached from the past, the mythic, and the sacred, and void also of any future, modern existence is suggested in "Pale Horse, Pale Rider" by a small dance-hall Miranda and Adam frequent, a sort of present hell tightly circumscribed by the suffering and death momently threatened by the story's pervasive background of war and epidemic:

> It was a tawdry little place, crowded and hot and full of smoke, but there was nothing better. . . . This is what we have, Adam and I, this is all we're going to get, this is the way it is with us. She wanted to say, "Adam, come out of your dream and listen to me. I have pains in my chest and my head and my heart and they're real. I am in pain all over, and you are in such danger as I can't bear to think about, and why can we not save each other?"

Such salvation as Miranda desires, however, requires some reconciliation, as in *The Old Order,* of the personal and the mythic—

there represented by the natural rabbit and by the patterned dove, here by the promise made to herself and the promise (of an apparently Christian life beyond life) made to her long ago. In "Pale Horse, Pale Rider" both promises depend on Adam and the question of his final absence or final presence.

—George Cheatham, "Death and Repetition in Porter's Miranda Stories," *American Literature* 61, no. 4 (December 1989): pp. 620–21.

JANIS P. STOUT ON MIRANDA'S HOME

[Janis P. Stout is a professor of English at Texas A&M University. Her works include the novels *Home Truth, Eighteen Holes,* and *A Family Likeness.* In this excerpt, Stout speaks on the theme of estrangement from home in the story.]

The most death-haunted of all is "Pale Horse, Pale Rider," another story with intertwined motifs of estrangement and yearning for home. The story begins with a sense of the unfamiliar familiar: lying asleep, Miranda feels that she is "in her bed, but not in the bed she had lain down in a few hours since, and the room was not the same but it was a room she had known somewhere." Her dream has taken her back to her early home in Texas, where her life was entwined with the lives of others in her family. In her dream she needs to "get up and go while they are all quiet." "They" are not the residents of the boardinghouse where she lay down, but her childhood family. Even her physical possessions are displaced from familiarity; they "have a will of their own in this place and hide where they like." Although "this place" might logically be the boardinghouse, where possessions would be hastily put away in temporary accommodations, it is apparently the place of the dream—home. The new place and the old are elided, and the old place, Miranda's childhood home, begins to seem less secure, less stable, than it once seemed.

In this first of several dreams, Miranda feels an urgency to get away before people wake up and begin to press questions on her. The intrusiveness of the family impels her to leave home even though she has "loved this house in the morning before we are all awake and tangled together like badly cast fishing lines." To assert herself, she must escape the entangling family by leaving home. Choosing a horse, one of the several whose names we recognize from the Miranda stories of the family past, she gallops away in the company of a thin, pale stranger. To make the essential step of leaving home is to start on a journey to death. This time, she pulls up her horse and lets the spectral stranger, Death, who is actually "no stranger"—he is a familiar visitor at home and joined her there, not somewhere on the road—ride on alone. But she knows she will go the distance with him another time.

Miranda's second dream, after she falls ill with flu, also involves vestiges of home, though home—Texas—is not specified. It is simply "another place she had known first and loved best," a place of "cedar, dark shadows and a sky that warmed without dazzling," "the spacious hovering of buzzards overhead" (a detail Porter mentions in "'Noon Wine': The Sources"), and a "broad tranquil river," plausibly the Brazos—again, a vision of home without the complication of people. But again that vision slides into death, a jungle of screams and threatening beasts and sulfurous rot, where voices cry out, "Danger, danger, danger," and "War, war, war." Once again the familiar shades into the unfamiliar, and nostalgia into fear.

Until hospital space can be found for Miranda, Adam, her doomed sweetheart, takes care of her in her room, and they talk about the past. Among the recollections they share is a song about death, "Pale horse, pale rider, done taken my lover away," which they had both heard in Texas, he in an oil field, she in a cotton field. Again, home and death, nostalgia and resistance, are linked. As Miranda drifts into sleep, she dreams once more of death. This time it is a premonitory dream of Adam's death, a premonition which will be fulfilled by the end of the story.

—Janis P. Stout, "Estranging Texas: Porter and the Distance from Home," in *Katherine Anne Porter and Texas: An Uneasy Relationship*, eds. Clinton Machann and William Bedford Clark (College Station: Texas A&M University Press): pp. 95–97.

[Thomas F. Walsh was a professor of English at George-town University. His articles on Katherine Anne Porter have appeared in *American Literature,* the *Georgia Review,* and elsewhere. He is the author of *Katherine Anne Porter and Mexico: The Illusion of Eden.* In this excerpt, Walsh discusses Porter's relationship with her Miranda character.]

In a 1963 interview Porter described herself in terms which identify her with Miranda:

> It took me a long time to go out and live in the world again. I was really "alienated," in the pure sense. It was, I think, the fact that I really had participated in death, that I knew what death was, and had almost experienced it. I had what the Christians call the "beatific vision," and the Greeks called the "happy day," the happy vision just before death. Now if you have had that, and survived it, come back from it, you are no longer like other people . . .

Whether or not Porter believed her beatific vision, in the thirties she wanted to think of herself as unique, that her near-death was a sign that she was destined for greatness as an artist. As early as 1920 she wrote her father,

> I wish our lives might run along a bit closer together. But it seems to me that I was predestined to slither off the main stem. You know Dad I had from my cradle the born conviction that I was a person apart, and that life would not do the usual thing to me. . . . All my life has been a hideous blind mad struggle to break my shell and achieve to my destiny, and I am now just beginning to see that I was right, that I was not deceived by that inner conviction. I am an artist, a little deformed by my battle, and a little weakened by a long grinding resistance, but a living creating force, just the same. I was not fooled.

Like Porter, Miranda is "a person apart," who has survived suffering and near-death to become the "one singer to mourn." "Pale Horse, Pale Rider" is Porter's new spiritual, composed to justify her role as artist.

Yet other comments of Porter imply that Miranda deceives herself into thinking she returned from the grave, like Juliet, only to find her beloved had died in her service. Such deception is in the best tradition of romantic love, on which Porter theorized in a letter to her nephew in 1948. In "love at first sight," the lover is "instantly transfigured with a light of such blinding brilliance all natural attributes disappear and are replaced by those usually associated with archangels at least. They are beautiful, flawless in temperament" while the love lasts. "And when I have recovered from the shock" and "put my mangled life in order, I can then begin to remember what really happened." Porter concluded that this "silliest kind of love" was all her fault: "If one ever treats a man as if he were an archangel, he can't ever, possibly, consent to being treated like a human being again. . . . It begins to look as if I had never wanted it." The language here recalls Miranda's description of Adam, her dream of paradise, and her subsequent disillusion. In that light, Miranda's very act of idealizing Adam suggests that she, like Porter, "never wanted" a lasting love relation at all, although she, unlike Porter, is unaware of it. Porter claimed she once told a friend in Mexico that the man in Denver was the only one she could have spent her life with. "And he replied, 'Just think, now he can never disappoint you.' And I suppose if there is anything at all good about it, that's it, but it does seem an awfully high price to pay to keep one's illusions, doesn't it." Her sardonic Mexican friend may be an invention since he simply gives a twist to a brief note she wrote in 1921: "Her love affairs were always playful or tragic and she always believed them permanent."

If Adam resembles anybody, it is Eugene Pressly, whom Porter put off marrying twice before finally committing herself in 1933. Although she depended on and confided in him, she could not live without him nor with him for long, preferring to live apart as much as possible and write him long intimate letters instead. Brooding and taciturn, he inspired Miranda's view of Adam sitting in the restaurant, his "extraordinary" face "now set in blind melancholy, a look of pained suspense and disillusion." Among Porter's papers are photographs that caught Pressly in that mood. Like Miranda with Adam, she "got a glimpse of [him] when he would have been older, the face of the man he would not live to be" still married to her. Below the surface of "Pale Horse, Pale Rider" is another story of how Porter wrote Pressly out of her life. He went through a perpetual death of departure and resurrection of return until his divorce-death in 1938. He hoped to remarry her, but, in a letter to Mary Doherty (November 1, 1943), Porter made clear why his brief visit was in vain:

> He had got fat, a hard, red, tight sort of fatness, less hair, and his fea-
> tures all drawn into a tight little smirking knot due to the strain of
> keeping his important personality all to himself. I let him come to see
> me, and then was sorry. Such a bore. If he got anything out of Russia,
> I am sure no one will ever know. Perhaps not even himself. I said good
> bye with blessed relief, and hope he is gone for good . . . whoever it
> was I thought I knew in Mexico by that name has been gone for a
> great while now.

He had become Adam, if he had lived, aging *and* fat—a justification of the fear Porter felt and expressed through Miranda.

—Thomas F. Walsh, *Katherine Anne Porter and Mexico: The Illusion of Eden* (Austin: University of Texas Press, 1992): 190–91.

GARY M. CIUBA ON JOURNALISM IN THE STORY

[Gary M. Ciuba is a professor of English at Kent State University. He is the author of *Walker Piercy: Books of Revelations*. In this excerpt, Ciuba relates the role of journalism to particular themes in the story.]

The world of "Pale Horse, Pale Rider" has lost such an awareness of transcendence. It is appropriate that Miranda works as a writer for the *Blue Mountain News* because her profession typifies for Steiner the cult of immanence in the twentieth century. Journalism articulates "an epistemology and ethics of spurious temporality." Everything—from stories about World War I and the influenza epidemic to Chuck's sports coverage, Towney's gossip column, and Miranda's theatre reviews—is of similar and fleeting importance, all new for a day, immediate and imperative, and then discarded in favor of tomorrow's news. As its origins imply, journalism is the writing of everydayness. It celebrates what is here and at hand rather than what is elsewhere and enduring.

Miranda faces the utter immanence that Steiner sees exemplified in her profession when an aged hoofer whom she has panned in the morning's paper brings in the reviews of a decade ago to prove his talent. Danny Dickerson's querulous song-and-dance stages a poignant protest against the oblivion that journalism requires each day if it is always to be up-to-date. Since the oldtimer claims that Miranda's unfavorable article will discourage future bookings from agencies in the east, he implies that she has actually written his death sentence as an entertainer. Hardly having time to talk to the showman, Miranda hurriedly objects that her opinion really does not matter. The ephemerality of journalism turns what is so momentous to the performer into what is only momentary for the journalist.

Although Miranda dismisses the has-been too quickly, she is deeply disturbed by this paradigm of mortality. If her review records his decline over a decade, her very position as a reviewer seems to be a way of daily writing herself to death. At the end of "Old Mortality," Miranda rejected her family's romantic and anti-romantic views of the past and dedicated herself to the search for personal truth, for what George Cheatham views as a typically modernist faith in "the freedom of the unconnected present, the here and now of her own experience, of herself and her own world, apparently including death" ("Death and Repetition"). As a theatre critic she makes that quest into her livelihood by her candid assessments of a stage that is dying long before its buildings are finally closed by the spread of influenza. Having lost the transcendent grandeur that thrilled Miranda in the plays of her youth, the theatre of the plague-year also lacks the kind of feverish imagination that Antonin Artaud celebrated in "Theatre and the Plague." It offers neither old-time ecstasy nor modernist iconoclasm but only works that Miranda finds terminally monotonous and dreary. Reviewing such a theatre is itself an occupation fraught with fatality. Miranda's habits at work—her odd hours, excessive smoking, and random meals in unclean restaurants have exhausted her flesh. As she stays up late to complete her reviews before the deadline, she lives out her dream of racing against the pale horseman of death. Mortality is inscribed in every sentence that she rushes to write.

—Gary M. Ciuba, "Death and Discourse in Porter's 'Pale Horse, Pale Rider,'" *South Atlantic Review* 61, no. 1 (Winter 1996): pp. 57–59.

DARLENE HARBOUR UNRUE ON PORTER AND SIGMUND FREUD

[Darlene Harbour Unrue is a professor of English at the University of Nevada, Las Vegas. Her works include *Truth and Vision in Katherine Anne Porter's Fiction* and *Understanding Katherine Anne Porter*. In this excerpt, Unrue speaks on Porter's rejection of the suggestion that Freud's theories are prevalent in the story.]

As strong as the evidence is, however, of Porter's conscious use of Freud's symbols and ideas, there were areas of strong disagreement. Early on, anticipating dissenting psychoanalysts and later feminists, Porter took issue with Freud's view of art and the artist and with his phallocentricity. As Freud explained his theory of art as neurosis and the artist as a would-be neurotic, Porter chided Freud with sadness rather than anger: "Poor dear doctor," she wrote in a marginal note in *General Introduction*, "it is just not so simple!" But elsewhere in *General Introduction*, whenever Freud remarked on penis envy or on the castration complex in little girls or on females' wish to become males, Porter took umbrage, once countering Freud in a marginal note:

> I never had the faintest envy of a boy, or remember having curiosity about them; but they looked closed up, and I thought they must be very uncomfortable! I have never had and have not now any sense of inferiority as a woman. My sexual pride is very natural and easy. I belong to the sex that has the values.

Porter amplified this point in 1958 in a long letter to Edward Schwartz, who had sent her the manuscript draft of his essay "The Fictions of Memory":

> And that brings me to Freud, and your use of his theories in one passage on "Pale Horse, Pale Rider" . . . about illness as escape, "[Miranda's] opportunity to assume the active role of the male," and the note about the sailing away into the jungle (Freudian point of view) "a wish for the male role." To me this is so wrong it is shocking, and yet it is almost impossible for any woman to convince any man that this is false.

Analyzing this misconception, Porter continued:

> In the first place, there are so many women, and we have all heard of them, who wish loudly they had been born men, simply because they

have been taught that men have more freedom, in every direction. What they really want, I think, is not a change of sex, but a change of the limited conditions of their lives which have been imposed because of their sexual functions. They do not seem to realize that men are not free either, and exactly on the grounds of their sexual functions. The uneasy sexual vanity ... makes a man resent a woman who is his equal mentally or in any other way.

Porter addressed a personal pique here, one that she commented on many other times; her feeling of being regarded in a lesser light than male writers. But in spite of her avant-garde feminism, now clearly traced by a number of critics, Porter rejected the label of "feminist" for herself, preferring "modern" instead and identifying *feminist* with *political activist,* a role she considered incompatible with the purpose of the artist.

—Darlene Harbour Unrue, "Katherine Anne Porter and Sigmund Freud," in *Critical Essays on Katherine Anne Porter,* ed. Darlene Harbour Unrue (New York: G. K. Hall and Co., 1997): pp. 88–89.

Plot Summary of
"The Grave"

"The Grave" opens with a description of the grandfather's grave which had been relocated twice by his widow and then once again after her death. "She removed his bones first to Louisiana and then to Texas as if she had set out to find her own burial place, knowing well she would never return to the places she had left." Following the grandmother's death and the subsequent sale of a portion of her Texas farm, the family graves, which had been buried in this particular portion of her farm, had to be dug up and moved to a public cemetery, buried alongside the grandmother's body.

The narrative narrows in on the grandchildren, Miranda and Paul (ages nine and twelve, respectively), just before they find the empty graves that used to be on their family's property. When they spot the open ditches, they rest their .22-caliber Winchester rifles against a fence and move in for a closer look. They are struck by a certain sense of awe when they discover that these ditches used to be graves.

Miranda and Paul leap into separate holes and dig around in the dirt, looking for buried treasure. Miranda finds an object which looks like a silver dove, the size of a hazel nut. She tells her brother, who claims to have also found something of interest. They jump out of the graves and compare their findings. Paul reveals a gold ring, carved with flowers and leaves. Much to Miranda's surprise, he is as enamored with her discovery, which he recognizes as a screw head for a coffin, as she is with the ring. They trade gifts and decide to leave the area, as it is no longer their family's property.

After gathering their rifles, Miranda follows Paul through the fields, searching for rabbits and doves and other small game. The reader is made aware of Paul's intensity when it comes to hunting and his disgust at his sister's lack of sense about the hunt. She enjoys hearing the gun fire, she tells her brother, who suggests that she fire at targets instead of game. She says she likes running around in the fields.

The year is 1903 and Miranda and Paul's mother has passed away. The grandmother had apparently discriminated against her son Harry in her will and now Miranda and her siblings are not as well off as they had been. Miranda is characterized as a tomboy who has not been forced to dress properly since her mother's death. She has always been told by her father that she should save her nice clothes for school and dress in informal attire at other times. "She had been brought up in rigorous economy. Wastefulness was vulgar. It was also a sin. These were truths; she had heard them repeated many times and never once disputed."

The narrative moves from the family background to Miranda's sudden desire, while looking at the sparkling ring, to run home, take a good bath, put on her most stunning dress, and sit in the wicker chair beneath the trees. According to the narrative, her desire for luxury also comes from "family legend of past wealth and leisure." As she contemplates leaving the fields, a rabbit runs through the weeds and Paul kills it with one shot through the head.

They find the rabbit and Paul starts to skin its fur with his knife. While watching her brother strip the coat from the rabbit, Miranda thinks about her uncle Jimbilly, who used to make the skins into fur coats for her dolls. Though Miranda never really liked to play with these dolls, she did like the fact that they had fur coats. Once the flesh is exposed, Paul and Miranda realize that the rabbit was about to give birth. Paul uses his knife to cut into the rabbit's stomach. They stare in amazement at the "bundle of tiny rabbits, each wrapped in a thin scarlet veil."

The sight of these unborn rabbits makes Miranda think about the sights and smells that she has been exposed to throughout her life. She senses that she is slowly learning what she needs to know in life. As Paul and Miranda gaze at the bloody rabbit corpse they become noticeably uneasy. Paul puts the baby rabbits back into the mother's belly and throws the body behind some sage bushes. He makes it clear to Miranda that she must never tell anyone about what they have seen, as he would be blamed for showing her inappropriate things. She agrees never to tell.

The narrative goes on to say that Miranda never did mention this incident to anyone and that the circumstances were buried beneath twenty years of memories before they resurfaced. Porter provides the reader with the occasion when these events finally reemerged.

Miranda is walking through a busy market in a foreign land (probably Mexico, although the country is not identified) when a vendor holds up a tray of dried sugar snacks, each in the shape of some tiny animal. "It was a very hot day and the smell in the market, with its piles of raw flesh and wilting flowers, was like the mingled sweetness and corruption she had smelled that other day in the empty cemetery at home." The story ends as the image of the animals fades back into Miranda's mind and a vision of her brother at age twelve takes its place; "a pleased sober smile in his eyes, turning the silver dove over and over in his hands." ✿

List of Characters in
"The Grave"

Miranda is the principal character in the story. She is nine years old when the story begins. She and her older brother Paul dig for treasure in the empty graves that used to be on their family's property. They find a gold ring and a screw head for a casket. Paul shoots a rabbit and they realize that the rabbit was pregnant. The story ends twenty years later as Miranda remembers this incident while walking through a market in a foreign land.

Paul is Miranda's older brother. He leads her through the fields in hopes of shooting small game. He kills a rabbit and skins off the fur, discovering that the rabbit was pregnant. He tells Miranda that she must keep this a secret as their father would accuse him of showing her something inappropriate.

Maria is Miranda and Paul's older sister.

Harry is Miranda and Paul's father. He was discriminated against in his mother's will.

The Grandmother owned the farm where Miranda and Paul grow up.
✿

Critical Views on
"The Grave"

GEORGE HENDRICK ON THE STRUCTURAL FRAME
OF THE STORY

[George Hendrick is a professor of English at the University
of Illinois at Urbana-Champaign. He is the author of
numerous articles on American literary figures, among
them Washington Irving, Ralph Waldo Emerson, Henry
David Thoreau, Walt Whitman, and Tennessee Williams. In
this excerpt, Hendrick speaks on the importance of the
structural frame of the story.]

The action of "The Grave" is set in a frame important for the understanding of the story. The first paragraph deals, in a restricted way,
with the family history, compressing much of our knowledge of the
Rheas into comments about the many moves of the grandfather's
body. Grandmother Rhea of the fictional account had moved the
body first to Louisiana and then to the family burial ground on the
farm; but the family tomb in Kyle indicates that the grandfather died
in 1879, seemingly after the Porters moved to Texas. As the story
opens in 1903, the body is being moved to the public cemetery. The
last paragraph, recounting a scene almost twenty years later, comments on and extends the significance of the event.

The two scenes within the frame are seemingly simple. The children Paul and Miranda, on their way hunting, play in the empty
grave of their grandfather; Paul found there a ring and Miranda a
dove-shaped screw head from the coffin. After leaving the burial
ground, Paul shot a rabbit about to give birth; and for the first time
Miranda understood the process of birth. The limited point of
view—sometimes swooping close to Miranda, entering into her
mind, recording her feelings and emotions; at other times with-
drawing, increasing the air of objectivity; and sometimes shifting to
the point of view of Paul, thereby portraying him in more depth and
also giving the reader another view of Miranda—is particularly
skillful.

In a blinding hot sun that day as the two children were hunting,
they entered the burial ground and were awed when they saw the

graves. At the age of nine, Miranda was still largely innocent, seemingly little influenced by the terrible discoveries she had made earlier in "The Fig Tree" and in "The Circus." With the coffin gone, the grave was merely a hole in the ground; and she leaped into it, scratching about as if she were a young animal. The earth had a pleasant, corrupt smell, and she found a silver dove with a deep cleft in the breast; the grandfather's body had found no peace, and the children, after finding the flawed symbol of peace and innocence, went on with their hunting expedition. The ring Paul found in the corrupt earth was a gold band, probably a wedding ring, engraved with flowers and leaves, fertility symbols. They traded, and Miranda wore the ring on her thumb, literally because she was young and it fit there, but symbolically because she was not then ready to wear such a band on the correct finger.

They then fled the cemetery, for the land was no longer theirs, and they were afraid of being called trespassers. They continued their hunting expedition; although Paul had given elaborate instructions, Miranda's reactions were feminine when she saw a bird or rabbit, and she almost never hit anything. They squabbled about their shooting rights; Paul claimed the right to shoot first if they saw a rabbit or dove, and Miranda asked idly if she could fire first if they saw a snake.

Immediately after this unconscious Eve-slaying-evil and Freudian sexual image, Miranda lost interest in shooting; she became interested in the gold ring on her thumb. She was then dressed asexually in hired-man's hat, thick sandals, and overalls, the wearing apparel she preferred, since she had not yet had any feminine stirrings and since her father did not object—it saved her dresses for school. But the ring made her want to return to the house, bathe, dust herself with violet talcum powder, and put on her most feminine dress. Actually, this was not all she wanted to do: she was infected with the desire for the lost luxury and grandeur of the family, and the symbolic acts she envisioned brought her into this fantasy world.

—George Hendrick, *Katherine Anne Porter* (New York: Twayne Publishers, 1965): pp. 68–70.

[John Edward Hardy was the coordinator of graduate studies in English at the University of Illinois-Chicago Circle. He is the author of the critical works *The Curious Frame, Man in the Modern Novel,* and *Certain Poems.* In this excerpt, Hardy speaks on the thematic richness in the story.]

In its compact richness, its unforced handling of a complex symbolism not so much invented as chosen, its exquisite sensuous and psychological detail, "The Grave" is one of Miss Porter's finest stories. Its wealth of implicit meaning is inexhaustible.

But it becomes clear that the greatest treasure the day of the hunt yields for Miranda is not the man-made things she and Paul find in the abandoned graves. These things, the gold ring and the silver dove, they exchange but do not share. But they share the memory of the dead rabbit with her unborn young. (Miranda explicitly refuses to keep the rabbit's pelt, which ordinarily she would have taken to make a coat for a doll; she does not want any material souvenir of the occasion.) The ring, probably a wedding band, is associated with the dead past, something representative of the hold that her grandmother's essentially morbid spirit has upon her—that spirit of obsession with the dead that drove the widow to refuse to let her husband's bones lie in peace until they could be beside her own. The dove, which Paul is holding in the mind's-eye picture that comes to Miranda in the Mexican marketplace, is a traditional Christian symbol of the soul's immortality. But, of itself, it has little psychological power. The vitalizing image for Miranda is that of the baby rabbits, her long-buried memory of which is evoked by the sight of the candy animals on the vendor's tray. Emerging from the welter of her other sensations in the marketplace (which first woke a "dreadful vision" of the old graveyard on the farm), the recollection of the rabbits, and her memory of the communion she had with her brother at the sight of the little bodies he had delivered unborn into death, produce at last a serene and triumphant vision of life.

In its totality, and in the central image of the rabbits, the young buried in the tomb of their mother's body, the story acknowledges the mysterious interdependence of life and death. But the final thrust is toward life. The act of memory itself, the fundamental act of human imagination, defeats the power of time. But it is further significant that the controlling image here is a *natural* one. In Wordsworth's phrase, Miranda's days are "bound each to each by natural piety."

Whatever of continuing good, for the present and the future, Miranda derives from her experience on Grandmother's farm, stems not from any "old order" of a social and economic system, of hereditary property rights, but from the earth itself on which that order was built. The sacred center of her life, the source of her sense of a vital and significant continuity in her experience, is in the fields where she and her brother knelt together in communion over the beauty of the wild creatures.

The immediate source of the title for the series, as William Nance pointed out, is Tennyson's *Morte d'Arthur:* "The old order changeth, yielding place to new." But the oldest order of all is unchanging.

—John Edward Hardy, *Katherine Anne Porter* (New York: Frederick Ungar Publishing Co., 1973): pp. 23–24.

JOAN GIVNER ON PORTER'S ACTUAL EXPERIENCE

[Joan Givner is a professor of English at the University of Regina in Saskatchewan, Canada. She was the recipient of a fellowship from the National Endowment for the Humanities. In this excerpt, Givner speaks on Katherine Anne Porter's true-life source for the story.]

Against this unsettled background Miranda Gay is described, the first incident of the story showing her awakening sense of her own sexual identity. In tomboy fashion, she is following her brother Paul, who likes shooting rabbits and birds. As they wander about they come across the recently emptied family graveyard on the part of the land which has been sold, and they explore the cavity which until recently housed the grandfather's coffin. In it they find a wedding ring and the screw head of a coffin, which in shape resembles a dove. Paul is delighted to possess the coffin screw and Miranda the golden ring. When she places it upon her thumb she becomes suddenly aware of her ragged and grubby appearance and longs to be prettily dressed and scented and to be reclining in suitably female fashion in a wicker chair.

Following hard upon this incident comes another one much more unsettling because it focuses her attention not on the external trappings of being a woman, but on the physical implications. Paul shoots a rabbit, and when he slits open its skin he reveals an interior full of fetal young. The sight seems to Miranda to confirm something she has sensed for a long time but has not articulated fully, and the knowledge makes her tremulous and uneasy. The brother swears her to secrecy about the sight:

> "Listen now. Now you listen to me, and don't ever forget. Don't you ever tell a living soul that you saw this. Don't tell a soul. Don't tell Dad because I'll get in trouble. He'll say I'm leading you into things you ought not to do. He's always saying that."

In the story Miranda keeps silent. She has no wish to tell about the frightening sight. The actual events on which the story was based diverged from the fiction at this point. Porter did, in fact, tell her father what she had seen and the brother received a savage beating. Whether the exposure of the brother was motivated by vindictiveness or carelessness, it constituted an act of betrayal the recognition of which cannot have escaped her. She was always troubled by any act of betrayal, and her deliberate or accidental betrayal of her brother and his suffering as a consequence must have added considerably to her sense of horror at the entire incident. That it did so is confirmed by the fact that, after the story was published, her brother reminded her of what really happened and she was furious and unbelieving.

The rabbit incident is powerful enough to stand alone as a complete story, but Porter adds another dimension by placing it in the context of Miranda's whole life and showing that the effects of this small event are neither trivial nor transient and that the past is not easily sloughed off. She tells of Miranda walking years later through the marketplace of a strange city in a strange country when a Mexican Indian vendor shows her a tray of dyed-sugar sweets. Suddenly the sights and sounds converge to bring back to her mind, from where it has long lain buried, the memory of her brother and the rabbit. The memory horrifies her and the horror reinforces the frightening nature of the incident and shows the capacity of past experiences to lie dormant and make a sudden unexpected ambush.

—Joan Givner, *Katherine Anne Porter: A Life* (Athens: The University of Georgia Press, 1982): pp. 70–71.

[George Cheatham is a professor of English at Eastern Kentucky University. He has published articles on a variety of authors, including William Shakespeare, John Keats, Lord Byron, Joseph Conrad, Ernest Hemingway, William Faulkner, and Flannery O'Connor. In this excerpt, Cheatham examines the symbol of the silver dove in the story.]

Suppose for illustration we look at a single symbol, much discussed, from "The Grave"—the silver dove, a screw-head for a coffin, which Miranda and Paul find in an open, empty grave. The dove unquestionably symbolizes the resurrection of man's immortal soul through the power of the Holy Spirit. That is, after all, why people put such screws in coffins. But that's not the point. The point, rather, is whether that cultural symbolism functions in any way in the story. We have several possibilities.

First, the inclusion of the symbol could be coincidental. As I said, such screw-heads were used on coffins, and Christian imagery in general is so much a part of our cultural baggage that accidental allusions and unintended, possible interpretations are probably unavoidable. Second, the symbol might be a pretentious device to add a superficial sense of weight or depth to the story without any particular religious significance. Third, the dove might suggest a Christian meaning which the story as a whole denies. In what could be considered a parody of the resurrection, Miranda's grandfather has left his grave—but only to be reburied in a new cemetery in town. The old cemetery has been emptied, in fact, only because his children have greedily sold off the land, including the family burial plot, as soon as the parents died.

Finally, the symbol might suggest a Christian meaning which the story as a whole affirms. Miranda does recover the "treasure," as she calls it, from the grave, and the dove is emphasized by the story's conclusion:

> Miranda never told, she did not even wish to tell anybody. She thought about the whole worrisome affair with confused unhappiness for a few days. Then it sank quietly into her mind and was heaped over by accumulated thousands of impressions, for nearly twenty years. One day she was picking her path among the puddles and

crushed refuse of a market street in a strange city of a strange country, when without warning, plain and clear in its true colors as if she looked through a frame upon a scene that had not stirred nor changed since the moment it happened, the episode of that far-off day leaped from its burial place before her mind's eye. . . . An Indian vendor had held up before her a tray of dyed sugar sweets, in the shapes of all kinds of small creatures: birds, baby chicks, baby rabbits, lambs, baby pigs. . . . It was a very hot day and the smell in the market, with its piles of raw flesh and wilting flowers, was like the mingled sweetness and corruption she had smelled that other day in the empty cemetery at home: the day she had remembered always until now vaguely as the time she and her brother had found treasure in the opened graves. Instantly upon this thought the dreadful vision faded, and she saw clearly her brother, whose childhood face she had forgotten, standing again in the blazing sunshine, again twelve years old, a pleased sober smile in his eyes, turning the silver dove over and over in his hands.

I prefer the last possibility—that the dove suggests a Christian meaning which the story affirms. But can I prove the Christian element? Given the portentousness of that childhood day, the dove might easily be merely a personal icon for Miranda, inevitably associated with her brother, her youth, and the day she lost a bit of her innocence. Porter's words themselves, though, introduce the idea of resurrection. The memory "leaps from its burial place." And the initial vision of death, the baby rabbits, fades into a vision of timeless innocence, her unchanged brother, clearly associated with the dove. But is that the resurrection of man's immortal soul through the power of the Holy Spirit?

—George Cheatham, "Literary Criticism, Katherine Anne Porter's Consciousness, and the Silver Dove," *Studies in Short Fiction* 25, no. 2 (Spring 1988): pp. 112–14.

MARY TITUS ON SWEETNESS AND CORRUPTION

[Mary Titus has taught English at Georgetown University. Her articles and essays have appeared in such journals as *South Atlantic Review*. In this excerpt, Titus speaks on the movement of time within the story.]

Throughout, "The Grave" reinforces the inevitable movement from nurturing and fulfillment to violence and loss. The "time" of the story provides an example. Miranda and her brother have recently lost their grandmother; "the motherless family" is now doubly abandoned, "with the Grandmother no longer there to hold it together." The grandmother's death, though, means more than the loss of a second mother: it means also the loss of land and a house; the three are bound together in Porter's imagination. The published version of "The Grave" records only the loss of the land: "After the grandmother's death, part of her land was to be sold for the benefit of certain of her children, and the cemetery happened to lie in the part set aside for sale." Little more is told about this loss except that, significantly, the cemetery was also a garden: "a pleasant small neglected garden of tangled rose bushes and ragged cedar trees and cypress, the simple flat stones rising out of uncropped sweet-smelling wild grass." Yet even these small clues reveal the cemetery as a place of sweetness and corruption, containing the two sides of memory, the nurturing and destruction that surround the relation of mother and child. In a page once intended for inclusion in the final story, it becomes increasingly clear that the lost land contained not only the cemetery, but also the fruitful garden and the family home. The page, among Porter's papers, and headed: "To be added to The Grave," describes the children responding to the loss of the land after their grandmother's death. Here it is clear that, with the land, a peach orchard and the grandmother's first house were also lost. After the grandmother's death, when the children return to their former garden to gather fruit, they are humiliated trespassers:

> Something more than her physical presence had disappeared from the children's lives with the death of their grandmother. They puzzled over the loss of land, over the sale of the finest orchard where grandmother had planted her favorite peaches. Even the empty cemetery was no longer theirs. They felt like trespassers. . . . [T]he summer after grandmother's death, they remembered her Indian cling peach trees in the orchard that was now sold. The three of them went boldly, walked into the orchard and filled their baskets with the fruit as they had done the summer before. The woman who owned the orchard saw them from her vegetable garden nearby. She and her husband had been renters, sharecroppers but in twenty years' time they had saved enough money to buy the first old house the grandmother had built, and her first beautiful orchard.

Each image of loss corresponds to another: the peach trees, the family home, and the fertile land are all lost with the grandmother's "physical presence," and that loss recalls the earlier, more central loss of the mother's nurturing body.

The loss of the two nurturing women forms the context for other moments in "The Grave" when fertility yields to death rather than fulfillment. The first accompanies the young Miranda's movement into puberty. The ring Miranda finds in the grave carries all the complex interweavings of sexuality, marriage, and death that shaped Porter's own experience. "Carved with intricate flowers and leaves," the gold band links the fruitful garden with marriage: yet the children find the ring in a grave. Marriage and adult sexuality may be the source of life, but they are also closely bound with death, as childbearing brings both life and death to a woman. Miranda at first thinks only of the superficial implications of her own sexuality. Playing with the ring on her finger, she longs to shed her rough clothing, to dress and act like a "proper" young lady; she wants immediately "to go back to the farmhouse, take a good cold bath, dust herself with plenty of Maria's violet talcum powder . . . put on the thinnest, most becoming dress she owned, with a big sash, and sit in a wicker chair under the trees." But when her brother eviscerates the rabbit, she realizes that womanhood wears the double face of sweetness and corruption.

—Mary Titus, "'Mingled Sweetness and Corruption': Katherine Anne Porter's 'The Fig Tree' and 'The Grave,'" *South Atlantic Review* 53, no. 2 (May 1988): pp. 119–21.

Robert H. Brinkmeyer Jr. on the Conclusion of the Story

[Robert H. Brinkmeyer Jr. is professor of American literature and southern studies at the University of Mississippi. His publications include *Three Catholic Writers of the Modern South* and *Katherine Anne Porter's Artistic Development: Primitivism, Traditionalism, and Totalitarianism*. In this excerpt, Brinkmeyer Jr. speaks on the epiphany at the end of the story.]

In the epiphany at the end of "The Grave," Miranda recovers much of the wonder and mystery of life that she had lost at the conclusion of "Pale Horse, Pale Rider." Now about twenty-nine, Miranda has her visionary insight while strolling through a marketplace in a foreign country (apparently Mexico). When a market vendor holds before her a tray of sweets shaped like tiny animals, Miranda suddenly sees again a long-forgotten experience she had with her brother, Paul, twenty years before. Miranda's experiences that day had deeply disturbed her, giving her a brief and forbidding glimpse into what the future held for her as a woman, but in her revived memory of the occasion, she transforms the events into a celebration of self and memory.

On that disturbing day with Paul, Miranda's displacement from the world of childhood began when, after slipping onto her thumb a ring discovered in one of the family's graves, she immediately found herself inexplicably turning against her tomboyish ways and toward the customs of southern womanhood embodied in the family legends. "She wanted to go back to the farmhouse," the narrator reports her thinking, "take a good cold bath, dust herself with plenty of Maria's violet talcum powder—provided Maria was not present to object of course—put on the thinnest, most becoming dress she owned, with a big sash, and sit in a wicker chair under the trees. . . . These things were not all she wanted, of course; she had vague stirrings of desire for luxury and a grand way of living which could not take precise form in her imagination but were founded on family legend of past wealth leisure." Further displacing her was the sight of unborn rabbits in the womb of the pregnant rabbit Paul had shot and cut open. What had once only been vague intuitions of sexual birth now became disturbingly real manifestations of blood and death:

> Having seen, she felt at once as if she had known all along. The very memory of her former ignorance faded; she had always known just this. No one had ever told her anything outright, she had been rather unobservant of the animal life around her because she was so accustomed to animals. They seemed simply disorderly and unaccountably rude in their habits, but altogether natural and not very interesting. Her brother had spoken as if he had known about everything all along. He may have seen all this before. He had never said a word to her, but she knew now a part at least of what he knew. She understood a little of the secret, formless intuitions in her own mind and body,

which had been clearing up, taking form, so gradually and steadily she had not realized that she was learning what she had to know.

Miranda's initial fascination with the rabbits quickly faded under the pressure of this disturbing realization. Whereas she had first seen the unborn rabbits as "wonderful little creatures" and had felt "pity and astonishment and a kind of shocked delight," she now saw a "bloody heap" and stood "quietly and terribly agitated." So disturbing were Miranda's thoughts about what she had seen and felt that after a few days of "confused unhappiness" she let her memories of the day's events sink quietly into her consciousness where they became lost amidst the vast accumulation of other impressions.

Twenty years later, when the vendor holds the tray of sweets before her and she smells "the mingled sweetness and corruption" of the marketplace, Miranda's memory of the day, until then merely a vague recollection of a hunt for treasure amid opened graves, suddenly "leap[s] from its burial place before her mind's eye" to emerge "plain and clear in its true colors as if she looked through a frame upon a scene that had not stirred nor changed since the moment it happened." Initially, her vision strikes her with the anguish she had felt when the events had occurred twenty years before, but as her mind quickly contextualizes the events, striving to understand their significance in light of what she has experienced and learned in the intervening years, her disquiet gives way to wonder: "The dreadful vision faded, and she saw clearly her brother, whose childhood face she had forgotten, standing again in the blazing sunshine, again twelve years old, a pleased sober smile in his eyes, turning the silver dove over and over in his hands."

—Robert H. Brinkmeyer Jr., *Katherine Anne Porter's Artistic Development: Primitivism, Traditionalism, and Totalitarianism* (Baton Rouge: Louisiana State University Press, 1993): pp. 179–80.

Works by
Katherine Anne Porter

Flowering Judas, and Other Stories. 1930.

Katherine Anne Porter's French Song Book. 1933.

Flowering Judas, and Other Stories (enlarged edition). 1934.

Hacienda (limited edition). 1934.

Noon Wine. 1937.

Pale Horse, Pale Rider. 1939.

The Leaning Tower, and Other Stories. 1944.

The Days Before. 1952.

Ship of Fools. 1962.

The Collected Stories of Katherine Anne Porter. 1965.

A Christmas Story. 1967.

The Collected Essays and Occasional Writings of Katherine Anne Porter. 1970.

The Never-Ending Wrong. 1977.

Works About
Katherine Anne Porter

Alexander, Jean. "Katherine Anne Porter's Ship in the Jungle." *Twentieth Century Literature* 12 (December 1966): pp. 179–88.

Allen, Charles A. "Katherine Anne Porter: Psychology as Art." *Southwest Review* 41 (Summer 1956): pp. 223–30.

Bixby, George. "Katherine Anne Porter: A Bibliographical Checklist," *American Book Collector* 1 (June 1980): pp. 19–33.

Booth, Wayne C. *The Rhetoric of Fiction.* Chicago: University of Chicago Press, 1961.

Burnett, Whit. "Why She Selected Flowering Judas." In *This Is My Best.* New York: Dial Press, 1942.

Curley, Daniel. "Katherine Anne Porter: The Larger Plan." *Kenyon Review* 25 (Autumn 1963): pp. 671–95.

DeMouy, Jane Krause. *Katherine Anne Porter's Women.* Austin: University of Texas Press, 1983.

Emmons, Winfred S. *Katherine Anne Porter: The Regional Stories.* Austin: Steck-Vaughn Company, 1967.

Givner, Joan. *Katherine Anne Porter: A Life.* New York: Simon and Schuster, 1982.

———. "Katherine Anne Porter: Queen of Texas Letters?" *Texas Libraries* 45 (Winter 1984): pp. 119–23.

Gunn, Dewey Wayne. "'Second Country': Katherine Anne Porter." In *American and British Writers in Mexico, 1556–1973.* Austin: University of Texas Press, 1969.

Hagopian, John V. "Katherine Anne Porter: Feeling, Form, and Truth." *Four Quarters* 12 (November 1962): pp. 1–10.

Hardy, John Edward. *Katherine Anne Porter.* New York: Frederick Ungar, 1973.

Hartley, Lodwick, and George Core, eds. *Katherine Anne Porter: A Critical Symposium.* Athens: University of Georgia Press, 1969.

Johnson, Shirley E. "Love Attitudes in the Fiction of Katherine Anne Porter." *West Virginia University Philological Papers* 13 (December 1961): pp. 82–93.

Marsden, Malcolm M. "Love as a Threat in Katherine Anne Porter's Fiction." *Twentieth Century Literature* 13 (March 1967): pp. 29–38.

Nance, William L. *Katherine Anne Porter and the Art of Rejection.* Chapel Hill: University of North Carolina Press, 1964.

Partridge, Colin. "'My Familiar Country': An Image of Mexico in the Work of Katherine Anne Porter." *Studies in Short Fiction* 7 (Fall 1970): pp. 597–614.

Poss, S. H. "Variations on a Theme in Four Stories of Katherine Anne Porter." *Twentieth Century Literature* 4 (April–July 1958): pp. 21–29.

Redden, Dorothy. "'Flowering Judas': Two Voices." *Studies in Short Fiction* 6 (Winter 1969): pp. 194–204.

Schorer, Mark. Afterword to *Pale Horse, Pale Rider,* by Katherine Anne Porter. New York: Signet, 1965.

Tate, Allen. "A New Star." *Nation* 131 (October 1930): pp. 352–353.

Titus, Mary. "'Mingled Sweetness and Corruption': Katherine Anne Porter's 'The Fig Tree' and 'The Grave.'" *South Atlantic Review* 53 (Spring 1988): pp. 111–25.

Unrue, Darlene Harbour. *Truth and Vision in Katherine Anne Porter's Fiction.* Athens: University of Georgia Press, 1985.

Walker, Ronald G. *Infernal Paradise: Mexico and the English Novel.* Berkeley: University of California Press, 1978.

Walsh, Thomas F. "Miranda's Ghost in 'Old Mortality.'" *College Literature* 6 (1979–80): pp. 57–63.

———. "The Dream Self in 'Pale Horse, Pale Rider.'" *Wascana Review* 14 (Fall 1979): pp. 61–79.

———. "Braggioni's Jockey Club in 'Flowering Judas.'" *Studies in Short Fiction* 20 (Spring–Summer 1983): pp. 136–38

———. "The Making of 'Flowering Judas.'" *Journal of Modern Literature* 12 (March 1985): pp. 109–30.

Warren, Robert Penn. "Katherine Anne Porter (Irony with a Center)." *Kenyon Review* 4 (Winter 1942): pp. 29–42.

Wescott, Glenway. *Images of Truth: Remembrances and Criticism.* New York: Harcourt Brace, 1964.

Yanella, Philip R. "The Problems of Dislocation in 'Pale Horse, Pale Rider.'" *Studies in Short Fiction* 5 (Fall 1969): pp. 637–42.

Youngblood, Sarah. "Structure and Imagery in Katherine Anne Porter's 'Pale Horse, Pale Rider.'" *Modern Fiction Studies* 5 (Winter 1959): pp. 344–52.

Index of
Themes and Ideas